Fill Me With The Fire of Your Love

Carlote Bengemyer

ISBN-10: 0982184557
EAN-13: 9780982184554

Fill Me With The Fire of Your Love

TABLE OF CONTENTS

DEDICATION

This book is dedicated with Love, to my beautiful wife Dodie. Like me, Dodie grew up in an America where the One True God was honored and His ways were revered by a people having Faith in Him and His Providence to guide and protect us.

Like me, Dodie has witnessed the moral decline of American society. The once Mighty nation, where majority rule was the norm, not the exception, has deteriorated into a country of pathetic people; concerned more about being considered "politically correct" than "morally responsible" to both God and their country. It is our prayer and desire to work toward reversing this Apathy, and awaken the True body and bride of Christ into taking action to return America to the Providence of the One TRUE God!

In 2011, I lost God's most precious daughter, my wonderful wife, to cancer. She went through a five year battle with this horrible disease. She was a great help to my ministry, as she would proof my books for the errors which would find their way into the writing. One of the last things she did was proof Fill Me with the Fire of Your Love.

As this book is about loving others as Jesus loves us. There could be no greater example of one who lived that kind of powerful lifestyle than my Dodie. If someone did something to offend her, she would turn them over to God to deal with. Then she would go on showing them love, rather than allow her flesh to plot its revenge.

I had spent over 40 years of my life looking to find someone like Dodie. Although we were married just four years and three months, Dodie was and is the love of my life. My life was BLESSED by God in His allowing me to be her husband, even if only for a brief time. I will love her till the day I die, and if the Lord permits, throughout eternity. She was a most unusual woman of great beauty (both inside and out) and virtue. I miss her. But I thank God for every moment of my life I was allowed to spend with her.

I have written the story of our love. It is in a book called: Love Poems for Dodie. It is a story of the kind of love most only dream of attaining. For an encouraging and uplifting story of true love, get your copy today.

FOREWORD
FILL ME WITH THE FIRE
OF YOUR LOVE

For me this is a privilege to write a foreword to this book. I have been a personal friend to the author for many years. I know Carlote as a straight-shooter. When he speaks or writes, he will let you know straight with clarity what is his intention for you to receive. This book is filled with interesting stories aimed at helping the reader know how to handle their life encounters. The teachings in this book will be a most helpful guide assisting you in your everyday life; and especially helpful as to how we may gain the power needed to keep the eleventh commandment of God.

I know Carlote personally wants you to understand the blessings of God coming from results of the Fire which accompanies the Baptism of the Holy Spirit. Allow the words of this book to stir your spirit, causing your determination to endure the tests and trials coming your way. God has great desire to see a Bride worthy of His Son. This author is not only gifted in writing his teachings but also a prolific poet, expressing his feelings and understanding thru the inspired poems which come from his heart.

Each of us can appreciate all the guidance and encouragement God can give us, and the writings of this author will stimulate your heart and spirit to press forward. This book should be a study guide and a resource for Biblical inspiration.

Author, Carlote Bengemyer, is very qualified man of God because of his experiences, handling the word of God and demonstrating it to this world. The fires he has gone through only refines the character and thus produces wisdom. Let this writing be a resource to expand your effectiveness and usefulness as a true Bride of Christ in these end-times. My prayer for every reader is to become a more effective witness in our world of the life of Jesus Christ and His kingdom. Truly, this is our purpose as a Christian.

Dr. Gerald G. Derstine,
Emeritus, Chairman of Gospel Crusade, Inc.
Founder, Gospel Crusade Ministerial Fellowship
President, Strawberry Lake Christian Retreat
Founder, Director, Israel Affairs International

INTRODUCTION
FILL ME WITH THE FIRE
OF YOUR LOVE

The writings in this book came about in a most unusual way. I was contemplating one day on how so many of the messages being preached these days contain one or more references to the soon return of Jesus, our Lord and Savior. Hardly a Sunday goes by, without hearing of the many Biblical prophecies concerning the return of the Groom for His bride, which have been recently fulfilled. These are very exciting times we are living in, we are being told, and indeed they are. But still, something very important is missing in action.

What could that one thing be? The Holy Spirit asked of me, "Where is His bride? Where are the virgins whose lamp (temple of the Holy Spirit) is filled with oil (the Baptism of the Holy Spirit); and whose Fire (Love) is bright and alive in the darkness of the world? Look, said the Holy Spirit, and tell Me if you observe such a bride? Is there a bride operating in Agape' Love, one knowing how to love one another and others like Jesus, with unconditional love? Can you find such a bride which not only knows how to love on the same level as Jesus does; but is currently busy doing so within the darkness of the world?"

My honest answer had to be, no, I'm sorry, but I cannot find such a bride in existence today. "You have answered wisely and honestly Carlote. I am giving you the task of writing to the true body and bride of Christ; attempting to awaken in them their need to obtain the oil needed and the bright fire required to find their way to the Groom." Had I not already relied upon the Holy Spirit for the material I write, I would have been overwhelmed with the awesomeness of this assignment. So I gladly accepted, knowing full well, if I am but a humble and willing messenger, the Holy Spirit will provide the message.

I am also aware that many within the false body and bride, those sadly deceived by satan into following after "would be Christian" man-made religion, with its perverted use of scriptures, dogmas, doctrines, and traditions of pride and division, will both mock and attack me and the writings on the pages in this book. Those who greatly fear the presence of the Holy Spirit (because He is the Spirit of Truth, Who exposes the lies and twisted scriptures used by religion) do not and cannot bring fear to the heart of one who daily welcomes His guidance, seeking daily to walk within the Kingdom of God.

I am so greatly honored God has chosen to use me in carrying out such an important assignment. Am I better than anyone else? No! Of course not! God could just as easily have used a frog to do this work. Even then, many would still cling to the safety of empty religion, fearing to let go, and enjoy to the fullest, their restored relationship with Father God. Why? Because religion, which has great appeal for lifetime babies; has Jesus doing all of the work for you; while you do nothing but show up for almost an hour on the Sunday's when you feel like going to church.

Not so with relationship! Being filled with the Baptism of the Holy Spirit and Fire <u>compels</u> you to become the witness of Jesus to others, which He intends <u>all</u> who would claim to be Christian are to be. Also, it means having to seek from Jesus, the ability to become the kind of **believer** Jesus proclaimed His followers would be. We are to seek to know who we are in Christ; that we may lay our hands on the sick, injured, and diseased, praying boldly in faith, using the authority of Jesus' name, and see them made whole. We are to learn how to put on the mind of Christ, that we may cast demons out of others by the authority of Jesus' Holy name. Lastly, by having the Fire of Love within, we are to do those works even greater than Jesus did!

Surely we know religion cannot and will not teach you how to do such things. Why is that so? It is because they are lacking guidance of the Spirit of Truth. Likewise as bad, the followers of religion do not want responsibilities of attaining and having to use gifts of power, for the honor and glory of God. Laziness and accepted apathy are some of the great appeals of religion. It's really that simple. It is my hope I am able to reach hearts ensnared by religion. Causing them to decide to leave the false and powerless body and bride, and become a member of the glorious TRUE body and bride of Christ! Also, may the true bride become awakened to her duty and the power available to her, that she may be given the wonderful wedding garment by Father God, to wear at the wedding feast of the Lamb.

I hope and pray this brief introduction has grabbed your interest. As you partake of the messages contained within this book, may you be greatly blessed. It is but the first of three, which I have been given to address the <u>True</u> body and bride of Christ.

With Love, God's humble servant,

Carlote Bengemyer

CAUTION

This book is written primarily to the True Body and Bride of Christ. Its intent is to help awaken the Bride to move in the Power of the Holy Spirit, and the Agape' Love of Jesus; that she may be given by Father God, the Wedding garment needed to wear for the return of the Groom, at the Wedding Feast of the Lamb.

I have been warned by well meaning people, that some reading this book will see only words of anger, and may get "turned off" by its boldly honest content. It is feared that especially those newly born again, still "babes" in the Word, will become confused.

May I say none of this is the intent of the writings you will find in this book. They are simply a calling from the Spirit of Truth, exposing the powerlessness of "Christian Religions," which deny the presence, gifts, and guidance of the Holy Spirit in the lives of those seeking to be true followers of Jesus. Exposure of the lies, twisted scriptures, misinterpretation (intentional or otherwise), and the many prideful man-made doctrines, dogmas, and traditions which lead spirits away from the Spirit of Truth; is something which has been badly needed and is long overdue.

As we are obviously living in the last days of time, and the end is approaching. Father God, by His Holy Spirit, and through His servants, is putting out a call to reject religion of any and every label; to come together in the unity of Love, by the Power of the Holy Spirit, and share daily in the loving relationship which we were created to enjoy with God and one another.

To those who may be newly born again I say be not confused, <u>become</u> **aware**! Many truthfully teach, you must be born again. But due to their reliance on man's religious "prideful" ways (rather than God's holy ways – made available by His Holy Spirit), they fail to teach God has so much more gifts of Power to give you by His Spirit. I pray you will see the wisdom of abandoning man's religion, to pursue your pure and loving "relationship" with your Father in Heaven.

True Christians are not now, nor were they ever intended to be a "religion." They are the redeemed children, who are given opportunity of growing up to become sons, and daughters of the One True God! We were created to share in a loving "Relationship – not "religion" with God, our Heavenly Father. It is time the world had this **Truth** and its **Power** visibly revealed in the lives of the True members of the Body and Bride of Christ!

Those reading these pages and seeing only anger, most likely are seeing it because of their desire to cling to the comfort zone their "religion" has provided for them. In that comfort zone, God does all of the work for them. There is nothing they need do, except perhaps <u>sometimes</u> tell people, "you must be born again," with hope of reeling them in, to follow after their brand of "Religion." Otherwise, all they do is occupy a pew for about an hour most Sunday's, when they "feel like" attending church.

Not so in "Relationship" with your Heavenly Father. Particularly in these last days! Father God is looking for Harvesters, as the Harvest is plentiful. He seeks those desiring to win spirits into the Kingdom of God – NOT into the label of their "religion," with its misguided man-made doctrines, dogmas, and traditions of pride and division, not unity in love.

In closing, I must forewarn each reader of this book. In its pages you may find hope, or despair. You may get angry with the Truths revealed by the Spirit of Truth. Or you may become aware to the fact that you may be attending one of the many "false" brides of Christ. Becoming angry, your spiritual eyes will remain blinded to the truth. You may choose to vehemently condemn both the message, and the messenger God has chosen to use.

Becoming aware, perhaps you may choose to find a member of the True Body and Bride of Christ; a church where the Holy Spirit is welcome and allowed freedom to endue every member with Power from on high, to use as you seek to attain spiritual maturity. I'm speaking of the kind of church encouraging every member to seek after and receive from Jesus, the Baptism of the Holy Spirit and Fire (which you will read about in the pages of this book).

All I ask of each reader is to fairly read the messages contained within, from start to finish. Then ask of yourself, is this not truly a book written for the last days of time? Moreover, ask yourself if you are safely attending a church that is a true member of the Body and Bride of Christ. Ask, seeking the gift of discernment. This is all I ask of the readers of this book. As you ask, may you hear only the voice of the Spirit of Truth, giving your spirit the answer. This I pray in Jesus name.

I CRY OUT

I CRY OUT IN THE EARTH THAT TREMBLES
I CRY OUT IN THE WINDS THAT BLOW
I CRY OUT IN THE RAGING WATERS
IN VOLCANOS, FIRE, AND SNOW

I CRY IN THE NAME OF JUSTICE
I CRY FOR THE INNOCENT DEAD
WHY DO YOU LOVE AND SERVE THE DARKNESS?
MUST JUDGMENT FALL UPON YOUR HEAD?

I CRY OUT IN THE NAME OF BABIES
MURDERED IN THEIR MOTHER'S WOMB
HOW YOUR HEARTS HAVE HARDENED
LETTING satan LEAD YOUR SOUL TO DOOM

WHAT WILL IT TAKE FOR YOU TO HEAR ME
AND RESPOND UNTO MY CALL
TO A NATION THAT ONCE LOVED ME
I SAY: **RETURN TO ME OR FALL!**

I SPEAK NOW UNTO MY SERVANTS
WHO DAILY CALL TO ME
ARISE IN LOVE MY MIGHTY ARMY
GO AND SET THE CAPTIVES FREE!

HOW MUCH LONGER MUST I CRY OUT?
HOW MUCH LOUDER MUST I SHOUT?

WILL YOU SURRENDER ALL TO satan
OR BY MY SPIRIT CAST him OUT?

TO THOSE WHO TRULY LOVE ME
AND WALK IN LIBERTY
USE THE POWER THAT IS IN YOU
TURN THIS COUNTRY BACK TO ME

UNDER GOD YOU ONCE DID PLEDGE THIS NATION
PRAYER TO ME WAS IN YOUR SCHOOL
IN GOD WE TRUST WAS **BOLDLY** ON YOUR MONEY
AND YOU TAUGHT THE GOLDEN RULE

OH HOW FAR YOU HAVE STRAYED FROM ME
FROM THE TRUTH, THE LIFE, THE WAY
HOW MUCH LONGER MUST I CRY OUT?
REPENT! RETURN TO ME THIS DAY

FOR I YOUR GOD AM JEALOUS
OF THE gods YOU HAVE PLACED IN FRONT OF ME
IF YOU CONTINUE TO CHOOSE AND SERVE THEM
YOU NO LONGER SHALL BE FREE

HOW LOUDLY MUST I CRY OUT?
HOW LONG WILL I LET MOCKERY GO ON?
WHEN WILL YOU SEEK MY MERCY
AND REPENT FROM DOING WRONG?

THE TIME IS GROWING SHORTER
TO RESPOND UNTO MY VOICE
WHO IS YOUR LORD AND MASTER?
SOON YOU MUST MAKE YOUR CHOICE

From: 21st Century Psalms
Copyright 2008
By: Joe Callihan

CHAPTER ONE
THE GREATEST ATTRIBUTE OF GOD

Have you ever pondered which of all the attributes we know of God is the greatest of all? Could it be the fact that He is almighty, having the awesome power to speak things into existence; planets, universes and so on. Or could it be God is Holy? He is incapable of wrongdoing. All of these are wonderful attributes of God but can we relate to them? Who among us can speak matter into existence? Who among us is truly holy? We have all sinned and fallen short of the glory of God.

Therefore, I believe the greatest attribute of God which we can relate to is - God is love. Could you imagine the hopelessness we would be in if God were without love? Without love there would be no mercy. Without mercy, there would be no grace, and without grace, there would be no hope.

It took tremendous love for Father God to send His only begotten Son to suffer and die on the cross in order that our relationship with Him could be restored to a state of purity by the precious Blood of Jesus. God's love is referred to as Agape' or unconditional love.

Can we possibly give that kind of love to others? Yes! The love of God can be shown abroad in our heart. Jesus even commanded that we love one another as He loves the church (we believers). It really becomes a question not of <u>can</u>, but rather <u>will</u> we seek the power to give unconditional love to others? The premise of this book is to offer the true Bride of Christ the long hidden secret to attaining the power to love others with God's "Unconditional" kind of Love. As born-again sons and daughters of God, we have the means available to us to gain the power needed to love others just as Jesus Loves us. And we'd better start doing it!

✞ ✞ ✞ ✞

Can you imagine a world without love, mercy, grace, and hope? Yet even now it is happening right before our very eyes! Mothers lacking natural love and affection, are paying murderers to have their baby killed for the sake of convenience (abortion on demand). In the news we often see examples of mothers, who again lacking natural affection, murder their growing children. How about the senseless drive-by shootings of innocent victims? Or the homeless being beaten and forgotten by an uncaring "me" oriented society? All of these are signs of the last days; the times when the hearts of many shall wax cold (Matthew Chapter 24, vs.12)

We, who wish to go by the label Christian, should not possess a heart that is waxing cold. We who are capable of showing the same love and compassion Jesus did, must use and demonstrate to a cold world, one which is dying without love, that love, mercy, grace, hope and compassion are alive and well in the heart of one who is a member of the true Body and Bride of Christ. Those choosing each day to <u>follow</u> Jesus (not man-made doctrines, dogmas, and traditions of pride and division), and <u>dwell</u> within the Kingdom of God, not within the cold walls of a frozen "church" building.

It has often been said that love is its own reward. To the Bride of Christ love is the answer. Love is the mortar which binds our Faith and motivates the fruit we produce in edifying the temple of the Holy Spirit. Love is the Way of storing up treasure in Heaven; the Truth, which destroys every lie of satan and his demons. Possessing Agape' love within, leads to Life - abundant and eternal!

Showing Jesus we love Him, through the loving actions we give toward others is rewarding to our Father in Heaven. For we are living in the lifestyle He has created us to know and share. Herein abides faith, hope and love. But the greatest of these is love (1st. Corinthians 13:13). Notice the greatest is not faith or hope, but love. Because that is how our Father desires to see us live in our relationship with Him and each other. This is why all the law and all the prophets are fulfilled in keeping the first and second commandments.

✟ ✟ ✟ ✟

Can you imagine a God who spoke billions of planets, stars, and universes into existence being without love? We often refer to space (although filled with stars and planets) as being an "empty" void. But how void would we, His creation be, if God were not a God of great love? How void and empty are the lives of those not surrendered to Jesus. Distractions fill their world; distractions used by satan to keep them from coming to know the Truth, the Life, and the Way.

Almighty God, whose power is limitless, created you and me in His image. He desires to watch us as we make the effort through yielding to the guidance and wisdom of the Holy Spirit, become His spiritually mature sons and daughters, (John 1:12) and as such, share with Him and others, in a deep and abiding love relationship.

But what was our response to the free will God gave to us? Man fell into sin by disobeying the only thing God had asked him not to do. Just one simple thing! Yet God still loved us so much, that He sent the only perfect sacrifice which could redeem us in His sight, His son, Jesus. Only the sinless Blood of the Lamb of God can take away the sins of the world. Only the spotless blood of His Son could be used to seal the New and Everlasting Covenant God had made with man!

Our Father knows well the will of our flesh is in conflict with the will of our spirit. That is why not only does Jesus' sacrifice on the cross **restore** our relationship, it also gives to us, as we become born-again, God's Holy Spirit (His Pure, Perfect, and Holy Will) to help us have power over the enemy and become a witness of what the love of God can do.

It is the job of the Holy Spirit to teach us how Holy and Loving God is and help mold us into His image, as we become holy as our Father in Heaven is Holy. The very first way the Holy Spirit does this is to bear witness with our spirit that we are a new creation in Christ: the redeemed children of God. As we study the Word, He teaches and reveals to us knowledge of God's love in a tender, loving and beautiful way.

God Almighty, Creator of everything, including sinful man, **loves** us! He desires for us to be able to come boldly (not timidly) before Him in His throne room and call Him our "Dad." My friend, how much more tender and loving can God be? He desires for us to call Him "Daddy" He wants to delight in us. He seeks to guide and bless our lives, that we may know and live in an abundance of Righteousness, Peace, and Joy, while here on earth, no matter the circumstances. He longs to hear our petitions of sincere prayer, both for our needs and those of others.

How could we possibly want to deny our Father who has so much love for us? I know there will be those reading this chapter, whom the Holy Spirit is speaking to right now. Perhaps you may have gotten angry with God, because a loved one you prayed for to be healed, died. In anger, you opened your spiritual ears to the voice of satan and chose to blame God, removing God from your heart's throne. All the while failing to realize God's will is Supreme. Not realizing God's love for both you and the one you grieve for was and is <u>perfect</u>.

Maybe you are among those who have been deceived by that questionable lie of satan, telling you God can't forgive you – your sins are too many and too severe. Hear the truth; the Blood of Jesus was shed for you by **God's standards**, not the standards of your flesh or that of the devil. God's standards are all based in **Love**! While we were yet in sin, God sent His only begotten Son to make a way of forgiveness for us. (Romans Chapter 5, vs. 8) The question is: will you continue to allow satan to keep you from the Way, the Truth and the Life?

To any who feel the call of the Holy Spirit upon you to repent, please pray from your heart this simple prayer....Father God, I realize Your love for me is so great, but I feel so unworthy. I feel this way because of the load of sin and guilt I have been carrying inside of me. I happily and willingly choose right now to submit this heavy load to the cross of Jesus. By your precious Blood, dear Jesus, cleanse me now! Take away every pain, every feeling of guilt and unworthiness. Let me be born-again this very moment. Fill me with Your Holy Spirit, give me power to overcome the works of satan in my life. Even more Father, by the power and authority of Your Holy Spirit, let me become a witness of Your love to others. Use me I pray, to lead others from darkness to light, death to life abundant here on earth, and eternal in Heaven.

Father, I love you so! May I be a child of yours who brings joy and laughter to You each day as I learn to walk with You in love. By Your Holy Spirit, may I grow into becoming the spiritually mature son (or daughter) You desire to see me become. All of this I ask in Jesus name. Amen.

CHAPTER TWO
MAKE GOD YOUR FIRST -
NOT LAST CHOICE

How often have you or I said, "I've tried everything else, I guess the only thing left is prayer." How little thought we give to what an affront this is to our Father. It demonstrates how little respect we have for the gift of faith we have been given. As Christians we are supposed to be <u>believers</u> in the awesome results we can achieve through the power of prayer. **"Confess your faults one to another, and pray one for another, that you may be healed. The effectual "fervent" (prayed with faith - not doubt) prayer of a righteous man avails much."** (James 5:16). **"Pray without ceasing."** (1st Thessalonians vs. 17) Do you see the kind of problems we have with 1st Thessalonians 17? Most of the time we either are too busy, or find ourselves too lazy to pray unceasingly. When we've prayed once or twice and our answer does not come immediately, we easily give up. Other times it is because we lack "belief" that we are a righteous man or woman, worthy of having our prayers answered by God. This I believe occurs because too many are being taught man made religious doctrines, not how to know who they are in Christ. I am speaking from experience. It was not until I diligently sought the Holy Spirit to teach me to know who I am in Christ that I began to understand the awesome power of my prayers. I'm still learning both the power and the responsibility which accompany it.

Many a sincere Christian has been heartbroken and shed many tears over a father, mother, sister, or brother who has allowed the demonic spirits found in excessive use of alcohol or drugs to destroy their life. Today it's time to dry those tears! Now is the time to make satan and his demon morons suffer and cry tears! As **believer's** having mighty **Faith**, it is time to use the Holy name of Jesus to cast them back into Hell where they belong.

✟   ✟   ✟   ✟

You may be saying, sounds good, but I don't know how. Have you considered seeking the Holy Spirit to teach you how, by praying fervently and diligently studying God's Word? Others may say, "I'm afraid to even try such a thing. What if it doesn't work?" If your strongest desire is to be a non-**believer**, you are correct - it won't work.

Not because the name of Jesus lacks power, but because you lack mature faith in who you are in Christ. I say this not in condemnation or with pride. You see these were the same fears, worries, and doubts I had upon discovering what was expected of me if I am to truly be a **believer.** If I claim to be one who follows Jesus, I must show I am capable of doing the same and even greater works than those He did.

Let's face it; such news came as a shock to my nervous system. So I brought all of my worries, fears and doubts to the Holy Spirit, asking His help and guidance. He answered every question and removed every worry, fear and doubt.

But not for free, there was a price I had to pay. The price I had to pay was to have a burning desire to attain spiritual maturity. Spiritual maturity cannot be gained without working to attain <u>mature</u> <u>Faith</u>. How strong a **believer** we are depends on the strength of our Faith. "With what measure you measure, that is how it (faith) will be measured to you." The more important faith becomes to us while being tested, the more faith God will give to us.

This is where the big price tag comes in. For our faith to grow strong it must be used through being tested. Many refuse the price of patience required by the testing of their faith. The trying of faith works patience in those willing to learn to trust God alone. Patience in trusting God and waiting on His timing, not ours, is a sign of mature faith. We must ask in our daily prayers for our faith and maturity to grow. We must study God's Word and quickly yield our spirit to the guidance of the Holy Spirit. I have been learning these things daily for years. Still, I find I am only just beginning to learn who I am in Christ.

✟ ✟ ✟ ✟

Knowing who you are in Christ is essential to being able to cast out demons. But equally important in dealing with demons, or even satan himself, is knowing how to put on the mind of Christ. Just ask the seven sons of Sceva. They tried casting out a demon using the name of both Paul and Jesus. The demon responded by asking, "Who are you?" A few years ago, I would have been afraid the demon might ask such a question of me. If it did, I was prepared to set all kinds of track records, running away. Today, as I have been discovering who I am in Christ, and how to put on the mind of Christ, I know no demon would dare ask such a question of me. I would be prepared to give the answer he does not want to hear....with authority given me by Jesus Himself,

I would reply...**I am a Believer in Jesus, and by the authority of His name, I command you to come out and be cast into the deepest pit of Hell!**

Today I'm not afraid to say that, because I have no doubt, worry or fear of its truthfulness. I feel certain demons fear hearing it, because they would worry about and have no doubt as to where they would be headed next. Where worry, fear and doubt once occupied my spirit, the Holy Spirit has filled it with Faith. Faith made strong by putting on the mind of Christ, and by knowing who I am in Christ.

I would prefer first fasting and praying before having to deal with certain kinds of demons. But if the demon was to suddenly spring on me, before I had the chance to fast or pray, I can honestly say, "no problem!" Because I know GREATER is the Holy Spirit residing in me, than satan and every demon on earth and below! The Holy Spirit does not fear satan or any demon, so why should I? Especially, since each day I choose to walk in the Spirit. If I yield to walking in my flesh or the "would be" power of my own spirit, then I have reason to fear.

So how about dealing with illness? Is the doctor the first one you call upon for the answer? In some instances it is only wise to immediately call for the doctor. But what if you are waiting for an ambulance, or maybe personally driving the one who is sick to the hospital? Can you find the time to lay your hands on the one who is ill? Deliberately choosing to pray for their recovery in the name of Jesus; doing so as a believer; one knowing who they are in Christ and having on the mind of Christ! If your church is not teaching you how to become such a believer, there is a problem. The teaching of the Holy Spirit is being kept from you by powerless religion.

Some may say, "I'd do just as well praying in the name of Bill, Mike, or Fred. You who would say such a thing are right! You have proven that you do not know who Jesus is, nor who you are in Him. I know, sometimes medical help is needed to bring about a recovery. I know too that sometimes even after the most sincere prayers of a believer, the one prayed for will die.

In every case, the will of God must receive preference. I had my high blood pressure prayed for by several ministers and brothers in Christ. But in turning to the medical profession, it was discovered a gall stone had logged in my intestine, and was causing an infection, which raised my blood pressure. Had God taken away the high blood pressure, the gall stone and infection might not have been discovered until it had done serious damage. Also, whenever someone dies in spite of our prayers asking for their life to be spared, it does not have to be a bad thing. For the born again Christian, death is just one of God's ways of calling us home to be eternally with Him. The other way will be observed when Jesus returns. But whatever the case, each day we must remember to be ready. In Faith, making God our first resort in times of trial and trouble is one of the ways we show we are ready.

CHAPTER THREE

HOW A CHRISTIAN POSSESSING FAITH
SHOULD RESPOND TO TEMPTATION

(A Study in James)

According to the writings in his Gospel, we can see the Apostle James knew well what a precious and powerful gift was faith. He understood an equal measure of this gift from God is given every soul and spirit He creates. Yet it is the importance we place on this gift, as well as our desire to not just possess, but **use** this gift for the honor and glory of our Father, which will determine the size of any future measures we may attain during our journey in this world toward eternity. Want poof? "With what measure you measure, that is how it shall be measured unto you." God is a rewarder of those who diligently pursue Him. "Draw near unto Me that I may draw near unto you." Those having faith the size of a mustard seed, and <u>use</u> the trials and tribulations which satan sends our way (tempting us to lose our faith) to **nourish** that gift of faith, by trusting in God's **perfect Love** to see them through, will find their gift of faith will grow into a mighty tree.

Although there seems to be some confusion over James' early statement: "Count it all joy when you fall into different temptations." James intent was to tell us not to fear satan's attempts at causing us to lose our faith or fall into sin. It is a "joyful experience," simply because we can turn the evil satan meant, into spiritual growth. It is so simple really. All we need to do is **resist** the devil, and he will flee. We resist him by using our shield of Faith to deflect his attempts to harm our belief. Then we hit his head viciously and repeatedly with the Mighty Sword of the Spirit (the Word of God). As long as our **belief (faith)** in the Word we quote is **real**, satan, not us, will be the one hurting from this spiritual battle.

✟   ✟   ✟   ✟

O Lord, how long it has taken me to learn this simple truth! Today when satan tries to remind me of how bleak things are in my life, I tell him I live by Faith, not by sight. Get this satan! **"All things work together for good to those who Love the Lord, and are called according to His purpose."** When I speak with the authority only Faith can provide, satan flees! When I am tempted to fall into sin, (although I don't always act like I should) I tell satan, "I am a redeemed son of God, the Holy Spirit resides within me. I will choose to be Holy as my Father is Holy; because I will hear only the voice of the Good Sheppard Who guides me each day. I refuse listening to your voice. Now get your stupid butt back into Hell where you belong!" Guess what? satan flees! It's so simple and not at all difficult to defeat satan (Jesus already defeated him while on the cross). We need only to remember that greater is He within us, than he who is in the world. We let the Holy Spirit know we appreciate His presence within His temple when we seek His help and

14

follow as He leads. It's our **Relationship**, and not "religion" which gives us **Power** over the forces of darkness. It is our desire to love and please our Father which helps us **use** and **direct** this power toward our enemy, satan and his demon dummies.

The Holy Spirit does not fear satan. The same Holy Spirit Who resides within all who are born again. Why then should we fear satan? We are endowed with spiritual Power within. Yet so many do not know how to call upon and use it wisely. Why? Because they either are too lazy to learn, or have only been taught the watered down "Religious" version of the Gospel. Many never have been taught how to enjoy and strengthen their "relationship" with their Father in Heaven. Far too many never have been taught to seek the Baptism of the Holy Spirit and Fire.

James also desires us to know that the Power of prayer brought forth in Faith can calm any of life's storms. Just as Jesus chastised the Apostles who in fear chose to wake Him from His sleep. Remember the huge storm which arose on the Sea of Galilee as Jesus and the Apostles were traveling in a boat? "O you of little Faith," Jesus said.

James warns us not to be double minded when praying for deliverance. Being double minded is when we try to observe in our spirit that Jesus is in the boat with us. (What reason have we to fear)? Yet we still choose looking with our flesh at how desperate are our circumstances. With the eyes of our flesh we see Jesus is sleeping. We do not allow our spiritual eyes to help us understand, it is the Son of God Who is with us. We then allow satan to tell us, "surely you will perish!"

We tend to forget that Jesus (Who is in the boat <u>with</u> <u>us</u>) is God. So easily we forget we are the beloved redeemed sons and daughters of God. Asleep or awake, God's Love for us is perfect! He will send His angels to guard, protect, and minister deliverance to all who believe on the power of His name.

James also warns us not to look at fame and riches as the source of our wealth, for they all will perish and fade away with the passage of time. Rather than fame, we must desire that God may be able to look upon us as a good and faithful servant. We must seek to store up as our riches as eternal treasures in Heaven.

James speaks of abortion. Not the sinful abortion of human beings, which takes place because of the lust of the flesh. James speaks of how we can perform a spiritual abortion **on** the lust of our flesh. We must daily **choose** to die to self, crucify the lust and will of our flesh, and follow only Jesus. In our flesh we cannot do this. But if we start our day seeking first for the Kingdom of God to reign within our heart; we will find the Holy Spirit bringing us the wisdom and power to "abort" (by crucifying) the lust of our flesh.

James reminds us that as we look into a mirror, our eyes which are the windows of our soul should be filled with the Light of life which shines from within. This Light of life which God first gave to man when He created him in His image, withdrew when man fell in sin. (Luke, chapter 11, verses 34-36) A spiritual death occurred within our soul and spirit when the Light of life withdrew. But that same Light of life is restored by the Blood of Jesus (John, chapter 8, verse 12).

✝ ✝ ✝ ✝

All who are born again of the Spirit of Truth have within the ability to discern the evil lies and deceptions of satan. They have within power to choose to live their life in the Word of Truth. The Fruit of the Spirit can come forth daily in our lives. The Kingdom of God: righteousness, peace, and joy in the Holy Spirit, is the inheritance we attain as coheirs with Jesus. No longer are we a salve to sin, for we now have gained the power to overcome sin (Romans chapter 6, vs. 14 - 22).

This truth I speak is of the meat in God's Word. It is only understood by those diligently seeking spiritual maturity. When I had not the power of the Baptism of the Holy Spirit, and the Fire of Jesus' kind of Love within my spirit I had no concept of the spiritual power which was freely available to me. As many others wearing the label Christian, I was a very poor example of one possessing the power of a redeemed son of God. Very seldom was the Image of God seen in me by others, because the Holy Spirit was not guiding my words and actions. Neither did I bother asking Him to. I knew nothing of my responsibility to daily choose denying myself (dying to self), I also never made any effort to pick up my cross, crucifying the will of my flesh to the cross, by seeking only God's will to be done in my life. Yet deep within I desired to be a true follow Jesus.

"Religion" with all of its false man-made teachings was my problem. "Religion" had denied me knowledge of the wonderful power I now had available to me by my restored "Relationship" with my Heavenly Father. This made possible by the blood of Jesus, and through the indwelling presence of the Holy Spirit. Those in the world do not look upon those calling themselves Christians as the redeemed sons and daughters of God. But rather as just other lost souls wandering around in the maze of religion. For those possessing only "religion," not a powerful "restored relationship" with their Father in Heaven, this is a true assessment. Is it not time those in the world witness that the redeemed sons and daughters of God have real Power the world cannot understand or give?

✝ ✝ ✝ ✝

Of all the Apostles, I so greatly admire Paul. Apparently God did also as He used Paul to write a majority of the New Testament. In my prayers each day, I ask God to give me the desires of my heart. Is it any wonder my greatest desire is to be like Jesus? I seek to be able to do the same works He did and even greater works, as Jesus said we would do. I seek to be the kind of **believer** who may lay hands on the sick, pray in Jesus' name for their recovery; then watch as it happens! I seek to be able to cast out demons in Jesus' name, whenever the occasion calls for it. I desire to be like David, a man after God's heart.

I also desire to be like Paul in the ministry God has given me. I never sugar coat what needs to be said. I speak with a boldness which can only come from the anointing of the Holy Spirit. I never seek for this to be "my" ministry, but rather the Holy Spirit's ministry working through me. Paul declared his teachings were not with the enticing and deceitful words of man, but came from a demonstration of the Holy Spirit and **Power**. His motive being that our faith might not be based on man's wisdom, but in the power of God (1st. Corinthians, 2, vs. 4).

James points out that although all who are born of the Spirit of God have within the power to produce the fruit of the Spirit. In order to activate this power we need to become more than just "hearers" of God's Word. We must have within a burning desire to become "doers" of God's Word. Isn't it time for those in the world to observe the redeemed sons and daughters of God living daily in the Power they have through their restored "Relationship" with their Father? Isn't it time for those calling themselves "Christian" (follower's of Christ), to be like Paul; daily demonstrating the Holy Spirit and Power of God at work in the life of those who are "doers" of God's Word? It is the "doers" whom Jesus will call to meet Him in the Sky when He returns. The rapture will not include the "lukewarm" who are content with being "hearer's" only. They will have to choose to become "doers" of God's Word in the times of trials and tribulations, or turn completely cold, in an effort to save their flesh (Revelation, 3, verse 15).

Lastly in the first chapter, James warns of how <u>powerless</u> **religion** is. He speaks of the folly of pursuing "religion." Although the translators make it appear James is exhorting us to seek "pure religion," this was not his intention at all. How dare I say such a thing? Easy! Without the Fire of Jesus' kind of Love governing our tongue (as the 120 on the day of Pentecost); we have difficulty speaking words of love, wisdom, and encouragement to others - especially to our enemy.

Likewise, without valuing our "relationship" with our brothers and sisters, we will lack the kind of Love necessary to recognize and attend to the needs of the fatherless and widows in their time of affliction. If we fail to love Jesus as a bride loves her groom, we will not possess the desire to keep our self and our wedding garment spotless from following after man's religious doctrines, dogmas, and traditions of pride. Seek after the Baptism of the Holy Spirit and Fire! Do not allow any man or his religions keep you from attaining the power needed to be a worthy bride for Jesus to return for and claim as His own!

CHAPTER FOUR
THE HARVEST

As we know from God's Word the harvest field is the world. We have been advised to become harvesters. But there is something which I had never before considered about the complete work which harvesters do. That which is harvested is not left lying on the ground. The harvest is not complete until the harvest is placed in the silo where it will be safe from bugs and the ill effects of weather. Guess where the silo is for those spirits which have been harvested out of the world? That's right! Hopefully your "Spirit Filled" church!

However it would prove to be "fruitless" if the harvest were to be put in a silo infested with bugs. This is why it is so important your church be free from religion. The harvest eventually goes through a cleansing process, its nutrients (which are beneficial to our body) are treated with care and encouraged to become powerful. The cleansing process does not wash away the nutrients; in many instances they are enhanced.

In understanding this parable you will understand the important role your church must play in the life of the harvested spirit and soul. Your church should be the place of processing, where the soul receives careful cleansing, and the spirit is enhanced with the power of the Holy Spirit. Religion cannot do this as it is dirty, diseased, and totally incapable of enhancing any life. A church which is a member of the True Body and Bride of Christ, empowered by the Baptism of the Holy Spirit and Fire, must seek to be the silo which protects, cleanses, and prepares the harvested soul and spirit to go back into the world; enhanced with the power of God, offering others the opportunity to be "born again." Just as with food that is harvested to eventually become nourishment for our bodies, so too, the "new creature" must be able to bring the nourishment of God's Word and Power to those souls and spirits in the world which hunger for truth.

Can you see why so often I exhort members of the True Bride of Christ to banish religion from their church? The church consists not of the label of the body part you may associate with. The church is made up of those who not only **believe** on Jesus; they are actually willing to be servants who choose each day to **follow** Jesus as the Holy Spirit leads them. If each member of the Body of Christ were to make the effort to do this, every member would be able to see clearly. In doing so, they could help get the speck out of the eye of their fellow member of the Body by using the edifying power of Love. Those members which we think to be of less honor, will find us bestowing more **abundant** honor upon them; and uncomely parts of the Body will start to have more **abundant** comeliness (1st Corinthians 12: vs. 11- 27).

I hope you enjoyed reading this chapter. It's the shortest one yet! I almost feel ashamed to call it a chapter, but I am not ashamed of its content. I thank God for allowing me to share it.

CHAPTER FIVE
STUDY TO SHOW YOUR SELF
APPROVED

Often in this and other books, I have exhorted the reader to Study and not just read God's Word. I say this because in doing so we are more likely to become doers of God's Word. In 2nd Timothy, 2:15, Paul encourages Timothy to <u>study</u> that he may show he is approved by God as a minister who needs not be ashamed. Because he knows the truth regarding what God's Word says and means. There are some however, who take this measure to extremes. They study with their carnal mind as teacher, and it profits them nothing.

Some do this in an effort to show off their "great intellect," in hopes of impressing their listeners with the "depth" of their study. They will say things like: In the Greek "was" conjugated in the third person means "could have been." But in ancient Hebrew, "was" means "once did exist." Whereas in the Roman translation, it means, "you don't say!" The listener is supposed to be in awe, thinking, "This guy is so deep, he must have studied God's Word well!" Studied yes, but who was his teacher, Confusion? Would it not have been better, had the listener come away thinking, "Now I better understand how this scripture relates to my daily life."

Then there are those who study scripture, but sadly do so under the bondage of their "religious beliefs." In this case "religion" does not permit the Holy Spirit the "Liberty" needed to reveal the truth. Those in bondage to their "religious beliefs" will seek out only those scriptures which they can twist and bend into confirming their "religious beliefs." These are not interested in receiving any other scripture which might point out the error of any "religious belief" they hold dear. They will however readily slant scripture to support their "religious dogmatic stance." These very often are the ones opposed to making any effort to answer Jesus' prayer that we would be one body of believer's, united in Love. Their beliefs in self-righteous pride only permit them to attack and look down upon other members of the Body of Christ.

Those who are staunchly "religious" will not easily welcome to speak from their pulpit any who do not possess their same scriptural slant. I once ran across this when trying to obtain speaking engagements. My pastor, who was supportive of the work the Holy Spirit was doing in me, had taken me with him to several pastoral monthly meetings. He would introduce me to other pastors, and tell them how enthused he was over what the Holy Spirit was doing in my life. He would tell them how I was being used to write books to the church. I would inform each about my background, and give them sample chapters to read. I would then ask if I might someday be allowed to come to their church to share.

After some time had passed and I had as yet received no offer to speak, I asked my pastor why this was happening. I told him I clearly realized pastors have an obligation to protect the pulpit and not allow any false prophet to speak. But I told him how clearly the messages I have contain a power of anointing only the Holy Spirit could impart. His answer

24

shocked me. He said that in his denomination, unless you had a piece of paper stating you had attended their "cemetery," and were indoctrinated exactly with their way of believing, you would never be offered a place at their pulpit.

My pastor friend went on to tell me of another possibility. He said sometimes, when a pastor can see you have a powerful ministry, they become afraid of you. Afraid some of the members of their congregation might approach you, and offer you the chance to become their pastor. I told him they need never fear that from me. Being a pastor is not my calling. Were I to get myself tied down in one place, I would risk dying a failure to the work God has called me to do. Then with sincerity, he revealed his own motivation. He told me although he believed the teachings I have comes from the anointing of the Holy Spirit, he could not permit me to speak from the pulpit in his church. He said he feared that if anything I might say offended one member of his congregation, they might report him, and he would risk loosing his job. Isn't that odd?

Then there are some churches which will welcome any speaker with "celebrity." They will look more to the speaker's fame, rather than to the validity of their message. When these books get out, and become best sellers, I hope and pray I can avoid any wanting me to speak because of my "celebrity." My desire is to lift up the name of Jesus. I am only a servant, as we all should be. I will welcome any who would ask me to come and speak because of the content of the messages, their anointing, and their source. I indeed admit to being a different kind of writer. I rely on the Holy Spirit to be my only teacher and source of my material. When I attempt to study God's Word, I ask the Holy Spirit to reveal and teach me what it means, and how it applies to my life and yours.

The problem I generally encounter is having exposed "religious garbage." This is considered a no-no from many pulpits. I have discovered the devoutly "religious" churches are "confounded" by "foolish" speakers like me. It is understandable that those who have made their "living" by twisting scriptures, and just outright deceiving their "flock" into following after powerless "religion," feel threatened by one speaking under the anointing and authority of the Holy Spirit.

But Praise be unto God! We are living at a point in time when God is raising up messengers to the church. They will be used to give messages exhorting the Bride of Christ to be **ready**, become **worthy,** and put on a **spotless** wedding garment. These messages will go out - with or without a pulpit! This is why God has used me to address the church through writing books. It is also why the books are considered "controversial" by many. (Mark 7: 7- 9).

When I exhort the reader to study and not just read God's Word, I am encouraging them to ask the Holy Spirit to open their spiritual eyes and ears. May He clear away all "religious dogma" from their spiritual eyes, and remove the filth of "religious doctrines" which may be blocking spiritual ears from hearing the truth. Allow only the Spirit of Truth, Who inspired the writing of God's Word, to teach you the meaning of scripture. I refer you to the following: II Corinthians, chapter 2, verses 12-16; John, chapter 14, verse 26; and 1st John, chapter 2, verse 27. We must always seek to be a servant of God. One who exhorts others to follow Jesus, not by the wisdom of our intellect, but rather the power of the example set through producing the fruit of the Spirit in our daily life. Let us strive to live in the beauty and power of God's Word, as we receive the Holy Spirit's anointing upon a "foolish" and yielded vessel. In Jesus name I pray. Amen.

CHAPTER SIX
CALLING ON THE NAME OF JESUS

Just as I was about to waken I had a wonderful dream one morning. In fact after I had it and was marveling over it, the Holy Spirit instructed me to wake up and put it in this book. So here goes.

I was walking in an amusement park. As I walked past him, one fellow seemed to be not very amused. Suddenly he yelled out with an angry voice saying, **"Jesus Christ!"** "That's what I like to hear, I responded, someone not ashamed to call on Jesus' name out loud. What can He help you with, my friend?" I boldly asked.

"He can't help me!" was his reply.

"Well let's see, Jesus created the earth and all that's in it, the Heavens and all of the universes it contains; and just as you declared, He is the "Christ," the "Anointed One. So what little problem could you possibly have that's too small for Jesus to help you with?" (I just love asking questions, especially to a responsive person).

"Maybe "can't" is the wrong word," he answered. "Let's just say, He won't help me."

"But why not, I asked. Jesus was "anointed" by God the Father, exactly for that purpose, to help people like you and me."

With the sound of frustration in his voice he said, "You maybe, but not me."

I calmly replied, "If Jesus helps me, and He truly does everyday, then why not you?"

"I've sinned too many times! THAT'S WHY!"

"Oh, a simple little thing like that?" I replied. "Buddy, if you and I were to enter into a sin counting contest, I bet I could beat you hands down. But as numerous and bad as my sins were, I've discovered that no one has a corner on the sin market. But there is only One, Who has cornered the Forgiveness of sins market. I know you know Who He is. I just heard you call out His name as I was passing by."

"Do you really think He could forgive me?"

"No, I don't think so," I replied. "**I KNOW SO!**" In fact, there is only one sin which cannot be forgiven, and that's blasphemy against the Holy Spirit. Since you are here alive and talking to me, it's obvious you haven't committed that sin. All you really have to do is call on the name of Jesus, just as I did several years ago. Of course to be effective and get a positive response, you might try using a different tone of voice, and have a somewhat different attitude than you did a little while ago. But if you will call out to Jesus, with the same kind of passion as you did; you will find He's not too busy to hear and answer your call for forgiveness. I know what I'm talking about, because He did this for me when I called on His name asking for forgiveness."

This dream has a happy ending. I led the man in composing his own version of the "sinners" prayer. It was so sincere, and came directly from his heart. I can't wait to meet this man in real life, and see this "dream," become a reality. (I like dreams like this, wish I had more of them).

In the mean time, if you should happen to run across him before I do, feel free to set him free by the Spirit of Truth. Please don't leave him waiting for me. You are just as much God's representative as I am. Some may say, "but no one "elected" me to be a "representative." You elected yourself, the day you enlisted to serve in God's Army of Life and Light. Of course you have the freedom to desert, and go back to serving in satan's losing army of death and darkness. But if you love God and your brother as yourself, and don't want to be living among the poorest in Heaven, you will minister to your brother when you see him in need.

I know this chapter is short. But there's really nothing more that needs to be said, except perhaps a simple prayerful request. May God help you and me each day through the Holy Spirit, to be a FEARLESS and GREAT representative of Jesus, and FIERCE warrior's in God's Army. Amen.

CHAPTER SEVEN
LOOKING BEYOND TODAY

We have in our daily life today, family members, friends, and other loved ones, who have not given their heart to Jesus. Some we have personal contact with on a daily basis, while others may live far away. The Holy Spirit has taught me the importance of the example of Jesus' kind of love we offer to them each day. Those both far and near can be drawn to, or driven away from Jesus, by the way they see Him in our life style. When we allow our unruly tongue to say things like: "God may forgive you, but I can't," how phony must seem the label "Christian" (a follower of Christ), we wear proudly to church on Sundays.

So many are the opportunities I've missed to be a good witness of Jesus to my family members, friends, and other loved ones. I've done so because of my lack of understanding a basic truth. **The "Fruit" we permit the Holy Spirit to produce in our life, as we yield to His guidance, is very important in our today, as well as our tomorrow.** The spirit of our brothers and sisters will be drawn to

Jesus, as they can see Him in us, through the Power of His Love working in our daily life.

Those living by the world's standards are so drawn by their weak flesh toward the concepts of hatred, vengeance, and many other forms of darkness. All the while inside, their soul cries out against such behavior. I know this is so, because I used to walk in the ways of the world. I used to be so "proud" of the "power" of my flesh, never realizing how truly weak and stupid I was, regarding Real Power.

The only "power" darkness has is to steal, destroy, and bring spiritual death to the eternal soul and spirit of a man. In no way may "power" be attained by calling satan - master. The power of Light, Love, and eternal Life of soul and spirit, belong only to the redeemed sons and daughters of God. The highest form of Real Power is the POWER to Love others as Jesus loves us!

✜   ✜   ✜   ✜

The question each must ask is: which power do we desire to daily possess and use? Being born of the Spirit of God permits us to possess the power to bring forth spiritual fruit which gives honor and glory to God. But possessing, yet never using this great power, will not store up treasure in Heaven for us. Likewise, not seeking this power permits satan to direct the path you feel comfortable traveling on, and you can bet it's a wide path, leading to a wasted life. I don't need scripture to back up the truth of this statement. The kind of life I lived as a "Lukewarm" Christian, speaks volumes about the reality of our need for the Power of God to reside within, and guide our daily life.

Another question we must ask our self is: What will happen to my family members, friends, and other loved ones who die without having accepted Jesus as their Lord and Savior? To know and understand the answer we must pray asking, "Please Lord, help me to look beyond today." The day I prayed such a prayer, a stark reality was made manifest to me. It was so profound, its truthfulness made an impact on the kind of Christian I desired to become. The answer to my prayer, made me aware of the part I play in influencing the path others may choose to travel on.

Looking beyond today, to the day when Heaven becomes my eternal home and the Day of Judgment arrives, I became aware of a very profound truth. **Those family members, friends, and other loved ones who did not make it to Heaven, because they chose to reject Jesus and His Love, will no longer exist in my memory.** They will of course still exist eternally. But they will not be my next door neighbor in Heaven, as I had dreamed here on earth they would be. No, their eternal home will be in the pits of Hell, the home created for satan - whom they chose to serve over God.

✢ ✢ ✢ ✢

Sound too harsh for a Loving God? Not really! Our Loving Father knows the eternal joy of our home in Heaven would be incomplete if we had haunting guilt over the loss of even one soul we had dreamed of visiting with in Heaven. A Loving God will erase any memory we had of their existence here on earth. Only satan would desire us to harbor guilt and pain over one who had lost their home in Heaven because they in pride refused to give their life over to Jesus, accepting Him as the Lord and Savior of their soul and spirit.

Fortunately, satan will forever have no place in Heaven once the Day of Judgment has occurred. No longer will he be able to come before God to accuse us of our failures. On the Day of Judgment satan will be sent to his eternal home; along with all who willfully rejected Jesus and the power of His Blood to cleanse them from their sins.

Yes, in looking beyond today, I understand my role in the life of those whom I have the desire of visiting with in Heaven one day. I must be an effective witness to them of Jesus and the power of His Love. My life must illuminate the path I am traveling on; that it might draw others away from the dark wide path their life is on, which leads to Hell.

Within my flesh I have no power to illuminate anything. My flesh has no desire to bring forth any form of illuminating Light. If I were to allow him to, satan could use me to bring about a deceptive and false form of illumination. This is how "religions" get started by man. But fortunately for me, since I became born again, living within my body, soul, and spirit, is the Holy Spirit of God. The Spirit of Truth, Who brings forth a Powerful Light which drives away all the dark deceptions and lies of satan. This is why I must choose daily to crucify my flesh which desires to walk in darkness; and choose walking only in the Spirit.

✚ ✚ ✚ ✚

Whenever I find it a struggle to deny myself and crucify my flesh, I simply picture in my mind those whom I look forward to seeing in Heaven; the one's who have not given their body, soul, and spirit to Jesus. Realizing the example I allow the Holy Spirit to make of my life today, can very well effect their eternal home of tomorrow; it becomes easy to use the nails of righteousness, peace, and joy, and pick up the hammer of forgiveness. It becomes easy to crucify the will of my flesh, and pick up my cross.

You can spend your life's energy trying to deny these powerful truths brought forth in this chapter. Or you can let them affect your life, as they have mine. Your choice will direct your life's energy to seeking the kingdom of self, or seeking first the Kingdom of God to rule and reign in your heart. Any who would choose remaining "Lukewarm" please know my prayers will be for God to change your heart. Having personally been there and done that, my desire is to see everyone receive the Baptism of the Holy Spirit and Fire. Then <u>use</u> what you have been given to bring others to Heaven with you.

CHAPTER EIGHT

120 BACK THEN! SHOULDN'T THERE BE MORE TODAY?

Often when I've come across the words of Jesus in John 14:12, I have been both astonished and puzzled as Jesus told us (as **believers**) we would do the same works He did (raise the dead, lay hands on the sick, injured, diseased, and see them made well, and cast out demons – all in His name). Jesus also said that (as **believers**) we would be able to do even **greater** works than He had done. The word "greater" always left me questioning how can this possibly be?

First of all, I worried about God entrusting such power to man. Would we use it for God's honor and glory, or for the pride of self? Another concern of mine was how could I possibly have power exceeding that which Jesus, the Son of God had when He walked in the flesh upon the earth? For a very long time this power to do "greater" works than Jesus and why God would entrust it to sinful man, has been a mystery to me.

Only recently has the Holy Spirit revealed understanding of this scripture to me. First of all, God does not blindly entrust such power to man. If you read verses 5, 7, and 10 of John chapter 15, you will find only those **believers** who know His Word and **abide** daily in His Love, will be capable of such power. In the 3rd chapter of Luke, verse 16, John the Baptist foretold how Jesus would bring the promise of the Father, offering a greater Baptism than that of water. Jesus would baptize His followers with the Holy Spirit and Fire. This promise of the Father to give His sons and daughters power became available to followers of Jesus back then; and is available to all seeking to be true followers of Christ today.

Can you think of a work which the Father did not permit Jesus to do; yet encourages us to do? Through His teaching Jesus revealed many things to His Apostles and disciples. Jesus worked many miracles, such as opening physically blind eyes, and physically deaf ears. Yet never once did Jesus open spiritually blinded eyes, or spiritually deaf ears.

Remember when Jesus asked His Apostles, **"Who do you think I am?"** Peter answered: **"You are the Christ, the Son of the Living God."** What was Jesus' response to Peter's answer? **"Flesh and blood have not revealed this to you, but the Holy Spirit."** Father God did not permit Jesus to open spiritually blinded eyes and deaf ears for several good reasons. Had people been able to discern the truth about Who Jesus was, satan could not have motivated them to cry out saying, "Crucify Him!" Also, the Blood of Jesus had yet to make it possible for man to receive the Spirit of Truth to dwell within us 24 hours a day. The Spirit of Truth would bring to remembrance all which Jesus had taught and would lead us into all truth. However, as he was dying on the cross, one of the thief's next to Jesus asked, **"Lord, remember me when You come into Your Kingdom."** He received Jesus by faith, and perhaps was the first to have his spiritual eyes and ears open to the truth of Who Jesus is.

After Jesus was crucified, did His excited followers go everywhere proclaiming the "good news" about the Messiah having accomplished His mission? No way! They were afraid! Their spiritual eyes and ears were as yet unopened. Even after Jesus rose from the dead and appeared several times to His followers. Did they run into the byways, happily proclaiming the gospel? No, because they lacked the power and the ability to love their brothers and sisters like Jesus loved them. They were more concerned for their own well being than the souls of their brothers and sisters. They, like many of today's Christians, were in need of the promise of the Father: power from the Holy Spirit, and the Fire to Love others as Jesus Loves us.

Jesus knew they needed to receive power from the Spirit of Truth. The truth about Who Jesus is sets us free from satins' lies, fears, and doubts (John, 8: 31&32). Personally knowing our Messiah, understanding His Blood seals the new and everlasting covenant which God made with man. His blood restores within, the Light of Life, which must not be hidden from the world. (John 8:12; chapter 12: 36 & 46; and Matthew 5:14-16).

✚ ✚ ✚ ✚

These Apostles and Disciples of Jesus were much like the "religious" Christian of today they were lacking the power the Holy Spirit brings.

Like many of today's label wearing "Christian," they "believed on" Who Jesus is – the Messiah, Savior of the world. But without the Spirit of Truth to teach them, they did not learn who they were in Christ, and how to put on the mind of Christ. When the Holy Spirit is denied opportunity to teach these powerful truths; one desiring to be a Christian is left powerless; having only a form of Godliness – but denied the power thereof (the Holy Spirit).

The 120 gathered in the upper room on the day of Pentecost, as Jesus had instructed. They had been there for some time, in anticipation of the promise of the Father which Jesus had said He would send to them. We are told they waited without grumbling or complaining about the passing of time - they were in one accord. Perhaps the question had arisen, what could this promise be? Remembering what Jesus had said, maybe one of the Apostles answered wisely. "Jesus said we, His followers who believe in Him, would do the same works He did, and even greater works. The Master also said that we would receive "power," after the Holy Spirit is come upon us; and we would be witnesses of Him to Judea, Jerusalem, and to the outer parts of the world." All 120 were put into one accord by this answer. There were no "religious" debates about what Jesus really meant. Only excited anticipation filled the hearts of these **believers**.

Then the day of Pentecost arrived. Suddenly, there came the sound of a mighty rushing wind, the Holy Spirit had arrived, as Jesus sent Him to Baptize His followers. Cloven tongues of Fire also hovered over the head of everyone there as they received the "**Fire**" which had been promised to accompany the Baptism of the Holy Spirit (Mark, 1, vs. 8; Acts, 1, vs. 5, and chapter 11, vs. 16; finally John, 1, vs. 33 & 34).

✞ ✞ ✞ ✞

Having received the Baptism of the Holy Spirit, their spiritual eyes and ears were immediately opened. They fully understood all of the things Jesus had taught them. They knew beyond any doubt that Jesus was the Messiah, the Son of God; the "Rock" which He had told Peter He would build his church on. They **believed** the precious Blood of Jesus, sealed the new and everlasting covenant God had made with man (Jeremiah, chapter 31, verses 31-34).

Now that first small band of Christians (followers of Christ) had power the world cannot give or even understand. They were now capable of transmitting to others the Truth which set the captives free. But they also needed the Way (Love) to transmit effectively, and boldly tell others of the Life found in only Jesus; that others too might know the "abundant" (Spirit Filled) life which only Jesus gives.

This is where the **Fire** comes in. Having within the Holy Spirit, they were capable of making a huge impact on the world. But without the Fire, fear over their own safety would have kept them from using the ability they were now capable of. They needed the power to Love others the same as Jesus Loves us (John, 13, vs. 34 & chapter 15, vs. 12). In the 17th chapter of Luke, verse 33, Jesus tells us, "Whosoever shall save his life shall lose it, and he who is willing to lose his life shall save it." Again, in the 12th chapter of John, verse 25, Jesus indicates the spiritual value of being in the world, but not of the world. Lastly, in the 15th chapter of John, verse 13, Jesus speaks of how Love plays a part in making the decision to lay down your life for another.

What is the Fire? It is the motivation which gives us the ability to wisely seek bringing others into the Kingdom of God by loving them unconditionally, as Jesus loves us. It is the motivation and ability needed to keep the eleventh commandment (John, 13:34), the motivation and ability to love others the same way Jesus loves us. Just look at that first hundred and twenty gathered in the upper room. Having attained the Fire, no longer were the followers of Jesus afraid of torture or losing their life. They loved not their life unto death, but instead, loved others more than themselves. They were compelled by love to go outside and use the power and guidance of the Holy Spirit to open spiritually blinded eyes and spiritually deaf ears. As the result that very first day, the church grew mighty in the number of converts.

Indeed, many of the early Christians were put to death for their faith in Jesus. Always, they possessed the power to know the way to live, and the way to be able to die without fear. The early Christians were called followers of The Way. As we know, Jesus said: **"I am the Way, the Truth, and the Life."** For many years the early church was not crippled by being denied to live in the power of the Baptism of the Holy Spirit and Fire. The Christian "Religion" with its watered down gospel had yet to quench the power of following the Way, as the Holy Spirit guided.

The early Christians had not sold out to the lie, the man made teachings proclaiming the Baptism of the Holy Spirit and Fire was only for the Apostles to possess, and died with the death of the last Apostle. They lived daily in the power of the Holy Spirit and Fire. This power was so real in their life, they were willing to die if necessary, rather than deny Jesus.

Reject the lies of religion! That same power first birthed among the 120 on the day of Pentecost, is still available today! Jesus still desires to Baptize His followers; **believers**, who diligently are willing to seek this power in their life; with the Baptism of the Holy Spirit and Fire. Saint Paul received this power. In fact in the 26th chapter of Acts, vs. 17&18, Jesus explained this power to Paul. **"To open their (spiritual) eyes, and to turn them from darkness to light, and from the power of satan to God, that they may receive forgiveness of their sins, and inheritance among them which are sanctified by faith that is in Me."**

I realize there may be some readers whose "religious doctrine" has taught them to reject the possibility of possessing this power I speak of. Some may be screaming out saying, "No, you are being deceived!" To any who may feel this way, I would recommend reading Acts, 8, vs. 14-17; chapter 19, vs. 1-7; and most importantly, chapter 11, vs. 15-17. Having read these verses, seek God in prayer to lead you to a Spirit filled church, one where you may receive this same power in your life. Jesus desires to Baptize all **believers**. But only those **believers** seeking to follow Jesus, and not man made "Religion," can prove themselves worthy to be trusted with this power. For only by Loving Jesus more than your "religion" or it's label, can you offer His kind of Love to others, as you bring them into "relationship" with their Heavenly Father.

Loving others as Jesus loves me, is what compels me to make these books (which the Holy Spirit has guided me in writing) available to the world. I am prepared to receive harsh and unloving words of criticism, which modern day Pharisees and the "religious" crowd will direct toward me. I find my comfort in John, 15, vs. 18-22, and chapter 16, vs. 13-15.

My job is to inform every soldier in God's army that we are living in a new day of Pentecost. God is going to pour out His Spirit upon all flesh. Every soldier in the true army of God will reject every man made religious doctrine and dogma which promote pride, division, and seek to harm the Body of Christ. The Bride of Christ will be made spotless by the power of the Holy Spirit at work in her life. The bride will prove herself worthy for Jesus to return to receive unto Himself. For in the unity of love, the bride will be capable of loving others with the Fire of Jesus' kind of love.

Today-not tomorrow, every diligent and sincere soldier who seeks to receive from Jesus the Baptism of the Holy Spirit and Fire **shall receive**.

Then by love, we are able to hit those who are spiritually blind and deaf with the "Rock" - Jesus. Receiving the Truth about Jesus will restore unto them spiritual sight and hearing. This work which Jesus was not permitted to do, we, His followers, are given the opportunity of doing. It is doing the even greater works which Jesus said we as believers could do. We are offered the honor of restoring spiritual sight and hearing. Yet we cannot do this by our own power. It must be by the power of the Holy Spirit and Fire of Jesus' kind of love.

Just as the early Christians did, we will make a huge impact on the world as spirits are harvested from its grip. As with the early Christians, the world will respond with rejection and persecution. But through the power of the Holy Spirit and Fire, the soldiers in the true army of God will "Rock" the world!

Soldier, if you have not yet received the Baptism of the Holy Spirit and Fire from Jesus, please seek this great blessing of power today. With a hunger in your body, soul, and spirit, go after this power. Reject any "religious teaching" which would hinder your faith in receiving this gift from Jesus Himself. Let Jesus know of your anticipation of receiving the power to Love others into the Kingdom of God. Then pray and tarry in one accord with the Word and promise of the Father. Do not count the days, hours, and minutes. Count only the ways and wonder of God's Love for you and me.

Jesus, please give to all seeking to receive from You, the promise of the Father. This I ask Jesus, in Your Holy Name. Amen.

CHAPTER NINE
THE JOY OF THE LORD
IS MY STRENGTH

Times of tribulation can bring joy or sorrow in our life. It depends on the source we choose listening to in finding the answer we need. If we wish for the tribulation to become a curse, we chose to listen to and accept satan's lies. "God does not love us, He will not deliver us, and satan is our only hope." Accepting such lies, leads us to feel hopeless, we give up and give in to the tribulation, believing there is no way out..

But we who are the born of the Spirit, redeemed sons and daughters of God, have the free will not to accept satan's lies. However, this freedom requires us to use our gifts of discernment, faith, and the powerful Sword of the Spirit. We must discern exactly who satan is: the father of lies, the accuser of the brethren, and who we are in Christ: more than a conqueror. When we pray in Faith asking our Father for deliverance, we must be willing to listen to and follow the guidance of the Holy Spirit. Doing this will bring the answer to reality. (Ask and Believe, and you shall Receive). The Holy

Spirit will bring to mind which scriptures we may choose to stand upon. In doing so, we beat satan over the head, hard and often. his head will run back to Hell dragging the rest of his body behind. We attain victory when we are willing to fight our way out of the tribulation; not by our strength, but by the Holy Spirit's strength.

As you already know from a previous chapter, I have been going through many trials and tribulations. I thank God for each one of them. Not only has He delivered me from them all, but in going through them my spiritual growth has prospered like never before. I have learned I don't have to give in to fear and panic in the midst of life's storms, Jesus is with me, and I with Him. Jesus has shown me how to dwell in the secret place of the Most High. When we dwell there, we can abide under the shadow of the Almighty. It is found by simply grabbing hold of the meaning and truth contained in 1st John, chapter 4:18. God's love for us is **perfect** 24 hours a day. When you grasp the reality of that, and hold on to it with unrelenting Faith, you are dwelling in the secret place of the Most High. As you feel the comfort of abiding under the shadow of the Almighty, you will discover there is absolutely **No** reason to fear. God will cover you with His feathers and under His wings we can place our trust.

It is in allowing fear to take root that we choose no longer to dwell in the secret place of the Most High. When we open our spiritual ears to receive satan's lies, we stop abiding under the shadow of the Almighty. When we place our faith in satan or our flesh providing the answer, we tell God we no longer wish to be covered by His feathers and stay under His wings.

Our daily life is filled with choices we must make: Faith or fear, Love or hate, Forgive or hold a grudge, Ask for Forgiveness or be too proud, Live in Joy Unspeakable or in despair, depression, and sorrow. Each of these, are choices we must make throughout the day. To make the right choices

46

each day, our life must be filled with the Spirit of God. As we ask His help to walk in the Spirit, the Holy Spirit will instruct us as to who we are in Christ. I have found it is so very important to start off each day as Jesus instructed us to do if we wish to be a Christian - a follower of Christ. Everyday upon awakening, I try to remember to start my day with a simple yet powerful prayer. I will share it with you at the end of this chapter. But now it is time to speak of the source of the power of Joy.

If you will read the Gospel of John, chapter 15, verses 1-12, you will find our source of joy is found in abiding in Jesus, having His Living Word abiding within us. How? By our effort to <u>study</u> and not just read God's Word, and through <u>listening</u> to and <u>recognizing</u> the voice of the Holy Spirit. It's so nice to experience Joy in the midst of trying times. However, we can also experience excessive Joy in other ways. When we are willing to bring forth much fruit for our Father's honor and glory (through obeying the guidance of the Holy Spirit); and when we happily give Jesus' kind of love to others (through seeking the "FIRE" of Love to guide our tongue and our motives in what we do); we can experience Joy Unspeakable and Full of Glory.

Paul and Silas were in a dark and damp prison cell. They were in chains behind a locked cell door. What did they do? They sang songs of praise to God, with "Joy," and not fear, defeat or despair in their voice. What happened next? An earthquake occurred and the chains fell off, then the cell door popped open. Wow! But most importantly, the jailer and his entire family got saved. You and I need to be that kind of witness to others. I used to love it when a fellow worker would to come up to me and ask, "why are you always so happy?" Sometimes it was, "why are you always wearing a smile?" What an opportunity to tell them about my relationship with Jesus and the infilling power of the Holy Spirit. But sadly, on many of those occasions, I failed to tell of Jesus and His Love.

So you see I haven't arrived yet, there is still much I need to learn. I have however found a great place to learn, it's called God's Word, especially in the 15th and 16th chapters of the Gospel of John. What wonderful truths are found there. If you will allow the Holy Spirit to reveal their meaning, plant it within your soul and spirit, and nurture it by faith; you will understand better the source of your strength. When satan tries to steal your joy, you will find yourself singing songs of praise to God. Do you realize how badly this reaction hurts satan? he tries his best to steal away your source of strength, by bringing trials and tribulation into your life. For his effort, he gets to hear echoes of your praises to God, following him all the way back to Hell as he flees.

Jesus told us the things He has spoken were to let His Joy remain in us, that our Joy might be full. My Joy is full, whenever I am able to defeat satan's plans to kill, steal, and destroy my relationship with my Heavenly Father, or my neighbor's relationship with Father God or me.

I have found in going through tribulations sometimes lasting a year or more (some even ongoing as I write this), the Joy of the Lord is **always** available to me. All I need to do is pray in faith believing, then shortly I will be receiving. Receiving what? Skill in using the awesome Sword of the Spirit. I love to beat satan's head with the Truth of God's Living Word, which I proclaim to be alive within my soul and spirit. How often I have quoted from Romans, chapter 8, verses 28-31, and verses 35-39! The Joy part comes when I realize that with every fiber of my being, I **believe** the meaning of each Word in the scriptures I am quoting. In other words, I am not just speaking words to satan. I am experiencing the Living Word of God quickening my body, soul, and spirit; as I boldly proclaim the Truth to satan and demand him to take his lies back to Hell with him.

My brothers and sisters, the Joy of the Lord will remain in you when you learn to develop a tenacious, bull dog like appreciation for the Truth. What is the Truth? 1) God's Love for you and I is <u>perfect</u> - 24 hours a day. 2) <u>Nothing</u> can separate us from the Love of God, which is in Christ Jesus our Lord. 3) We as **believers** have <u>POWER</u> available to us which the world does not have, know, or understand. 4) When we diligently seek to <u>know</u> who we are in Christ, we need never fear satan, he will live in fear of us. The Truth is so simple and yet so powerful. Through daily crucifying the will of our flesh to yield our spirit to the guidance of the Holy Spirit, we can learn to put on the mind of Christ. We as **believers**, can do the same kind of works Jesus did. Moreover, in daily seeking the "Fire" which accompanies the Baptism of the Holy Spirit, we can truly learn how to love others as Jesus Loves us.

satan does not want you to know of these Truths, or **believe** in their **power** for your life. he uses religion, full of watered down Gospel, and twisted, half truth scriptures, to keep the "Lukewarm" in that state of want. Many perish for lack of knowledge. So many will find they have earned only eternal poverty in Heaven, because of their life's desire to follow a comfortable "You do nothing for God, He does everything for you," kind of "religion."

✝ ✝ ✝ ✝

satan loves Christian's who are no threat to his kingdom. he delights in Christian's who's Joy he can easily steal away, because of their lack of effort to learn the truth and how to stand upon it. Please listen to me **I am not condemning any individual.** Not that long ago I used to be in the very same condition. I am trying to very clearly point out the danger of following after "religion," rather than the growth of your powerful **relationship** as the redeemed son or daughter of the One True Living God! The modern day Pharisees within the church are going to be furious at me for stating this Truth so factually. I'm supposed to be afraid of them, and sugarcoat anything which may be hard to swallow. Too bad! So sad! I fear only God!

The job and responsibility God has given me is to present the Truth to you. It is by the Spirit of Truth I do this. The Power of God is **Not** found in **Religion**! The Power of God is given to you and me as we make the daily effort to deepen our Loving Relationship with Father God, Jesus, and The Holy Spirit. The Kingdom of God consists of : Righteousness, Peace, and Joy **in the Holy Spirit, Who dwells within us.** Living in Righteousness, Peace, and Joy, simply requires us to submit our daily life to the guidance of the Holy Spirit; and not to a bunch of man made doctrines, dogmas, or traditions of pride and division. The Holy Spirit will teach all we need to know, and guide the seeking heart into <u>all</u> Truth (John, 14:26).

Some will accuse me of wanting to tear down the Body of Christ, in offering such teaching from the Word of God. However, the Holy Spirit wishes to use me to "edify" the Body of Christ, and help prepare the Bride of Christ to receive it's Groom. I hope every reader understands I cannot make such a bold statement, without having received from the Holy Spirit the anointing and authority to do so. It is with awesome fear (the reverential fear, which we are supposed to have), of the huge responsibility helping prepare the Bride of Christ is. With humbleness, I as a member of the Bride equally am in need of what the Holy Spirit is using me to share. The only way I am able to successfully work toward this goal is to rely <u>totally</u> on the Holy Spirit for direction.

I have no desire to do or say anything which would remove His anointing on my life. To any and every critic I give this to consider. Had I failed to offer scriptures to back up every bold statement, you <u>would</u> indeed have reason to find a problem with me. But as you can readily find scriptures for each bold statement, <u>your</u> <u>problem</u> is not with me, but with the Word of God, and the Spirit of Truth.

I know some will say, "This poor guy has delusions of grandeur." I can easily understand such an attitude. Not too often in today's church has God given such boldness of speech to His servant. No one is more shook up than I am! But to any believing this toward me, I have Good News to share with you. I **know** who I am! I am a <u>foolish</u> <u>thing</u> God has chosen to use for His honor and glory. I believe I may have been among the "most foolish" God could find. A man or woman who chooses to be found "foolish <u>for</u> God" in the eyes of critics, is capable of handling criticism from those who do not understand what a blessing it is, being found <u>by</u> God to be a "foolish" thing.

It is as I am learning who I am in Christ, that I become inspired to have the boldness to write without fear - the wrong kind of fear. There is a fear which will keep you from accomplishing what God intends for you to accomplish. I know this is so. For the first twelve years of my life, after the age of eighteen, I permitted that fear to keep me from answering God's call on my life.

I write not with delusions of grandeur, but rather with a heart full of thanksgiving. For God in His mercy has forgiven all my years of failing to answer His call. Not only has He answered my prayers to be used by Him. He is blessing me in ways far exceeding my wildest imagination. We are living in an exciting time. It will be a time in which the Bride of Christ will finally work to bring an answer to the prayer Jesus prayed for us over 2000 years ago. Jesus prayed that we would be one body of **believers, united by and in Love (His kind of Love).**

✟ ✟ ✟ ✟

A body torn apart by the pride of man made religious doctrines, dogmas, and man made traditions, can never be united in love. At least not until those things which hurt and divide the members of the Body of Christ are rejected by those desiring to be the True Bride of Christ. Let the <u>false</u> **RELIGIOUS** "bride" rant and rave – it will only be their folly exposing them for what they truly are! Jesus told His Father the purpose for His prayer for us was so the world would come to **know** Who He Is, by Whom He was sent, and WHY!

It is because of the weakness of religion that Christians of today are looked upon as just another of the world's confused "religions." How few **believers** are there, willing to cast out demons, or lay hands on the sick and pray for their recovery. Worse yet, how few are willing, or even know how to be an effective witness of the fact that they are redeemed son or daughter of God! Christian label wearers fail to make any effort at producing the "Fruit of the Spirit," a priority for their busy daily life.

I speak this in boldness, not in condemnation on any individual. But only to expose the truth of how powerless is religion. **Understand, not long ago this was me too!** But God in His mercy, through the Holy Spirit, has revealed to me a powerful fact. A truth which has profoundly affected my life, and I pray it will yours as well. The message revealed to me is a simple and direct one. **"THIS MUST STOP! THE TRUE BODY AND BRIDE OF CHRIST MUST MAKE ITS SELF <u>WORTHY</u> TO RECEIVE JESUS!"**

My voice will not be the only voice God will be using to edify His church to seek to come together in the unity of Love. But we must beware, for satan will have many false prophets using sugar coated words of deception to lead many from the truth. Yes, it is an exciting time to be living in. But it is also a time when everyone calling their self Christian, must diligently seek discernment daily. This is no joking matter!

Even if Jesus does not return tomorrow; your tomorrow may be your last day of life on earth. Are you ready? What will your testimony before Jesus be, regarding how seriously you chose to follow Him more than "religion"?

It's time now for me to share my daily prayer. It has made such a huge difference in my spiritual walk. It has taken me from being a lazy, uncommitted couch potato, lukewarm "Christian"; to being on "Fire" with the desire to please God, and bring forth much "Fruit" for His honor and glory each new day of my life. I pray it will have the same effect on any who choose praying such a prayer in their daily life. This prayer, is not "the prayer." It is a prayer which the Holy Spirit has taught me to say. He may have a somewhat different version for you. I offer to share it now for the benefit of any who might want an example.

"Dear Lord, this day I choose to deny myself and accept only Your perfect will for my life. Gladly I crucify the will of my flesh. Please give me the spiritual wisdom to see, and strength to pick up the cross presented me this day. Dear Jesus, by the Fire of Your Love may I produce much Fruit this day as the Holy Spirit guides me in following You. I refuse to listen to the voice of satan and his lying demons. Let my spiritual and physical ears be open to hear only Your voice, the voice of the Good Sheppard. Jesus, may Your kind of Love motivate all I do and say. Holy Spirit I surrender my tongue to Your guidance. Please help me bridle my tongue that only words of love, forgiveness, compassion, and encouragement come forth from my mouth this day. Father please help me to be like David, one who is after Your heart. How I would love to offer reasons for You to call me the apple of Your eye. All of this I ask, in Jesus Holy Name. Amen."

Praying such a prayer each morning and diligently studying God's Word, will cause the heart of the "lukewarm" to become alive with the "Fire" to draw closer to God and to please Him with your lifestyle. Every reader having the truths in this book presented, have a choice as to what you will do with its contents. The "Lukewarm" can desire to stay in that condition, and suffer through the times of tribulation to come. Or get seriously "Hot" in seeking to grow more deeply in Love with God; and in doing so, seek to Love both God and their neighbor. Those who already are seriously "Hot" about possessing spiritual maturity, can rejoice in what they have read, and desire receiving even more growth. Or they can be content where they are, saying, "I'm too full to absorb any more." I don't know about you, but I desire to know more everyday. I know I won't be made perfect until Jesus returns. But that does not stop my desire to be as filled with spiritual maturity as I can be.

My goal is to be a powerful Light of God's Love to all who are in darkness. I desire to be able to Love others as Jesus Loves me, and do the kind of works Jesus did, and even greater. Back when I was a Lukewarm "Religious" "Christian," such goals would have seemed ridiculous and unrealistic to me. How I thank my Savior for restoring my relationship with my Father, giving me the Baptism of The Holy Spirit and the Fire of His Love, and delivering me from "Religion." I realize those churches which deny their members knowing and receiving the Baptism of the Holy Spirit and Fire are not likely to ask me to come and speak. Although this saddens me, it does not surprise me. I believe it is so important to attend a church which recognizes and honors the power of the Holy Spirit, seeking for Him to instruct every member to seek His power, wisdom, and fruit in their daily life.

I would wish that everyone calling their self Christian were to receive the Baptism of the Holy Spirit and Fire. Then be taught how to appreciate what they have received, how to use it, and how important it is to seek even more. I may not live to see such a day, but I know it is coming. For God has promised to pour out His Spirit in the last days of time. The very fact that He has chosen to use a former "Lukewarm Christian" such as me, to write such powerful teachings, should be evidence that day is drawing near.

CHAPTER TEN
WHAT IS THE PROMISE
OF THE FATHER?

One day I asked the Holy Spirit, what is the Promise of the Father? I wanted to know if somewhere it is specifically spelled out in Scripture. Much to my surprise, as the Holy Spirit taught me where to look I discovered it is in the Scriptures many times.

We know Jesus is our promised Messiah. A promise Father God had made to Abraham for his faithfulness when being tested to see if he would be willing to offer his only son, Isaac. We also know by the blood of Jesus our sins are forgiven and forgotten, and we receive the Kingdom of God within when we become born again by the Spirit of God. Still, the Promise of the Father received by the 120 followers in attendance in the upper room on the Day of Pentecost was even more of a blessing than they could contain.

With all of the wonderful Blessings we may receive from Father God; until we seek and receive the Promise of the Father in our life, there are still spiritual truths and power we lack. For example, we lack the knowledge of how each day we may choose to enter within the Kingdom of God (The secret place of the Most High) to dwell there in safety from the world and all of its evil. Thus being in the world physically, we are not dwelling spiritually within its system of evil and darkness; but rather within the Light, Life, and Power of God's Mighty Kingdom of Love.

Furthermore, God's Will in our life is not made "perfect," until we have the power to love others the <u>same</u> <u>way</u> as Jesus loves us; that is with "unconditional" and "perfect" Love. It's **unconditional** because we forgive any and every offense against us by others; and **perfect**, because all choosing to live on this level possess no fear! (**"Perfect Love cast out fear."** 1st John 4:18)

✤ ✤ ✤ ✤

Those possessing the ability to love **unconditionally**, as Jesus loves are willing to face physical torture, even death if necessary, for the sake of winning spirits into the Kingdom of God. They know by faith and believe beyond any doubt, the price love demands is well worth the cost. As we are warned in God's Word, "label wearing Christians," who in fear wish to save their physical life by denying God, refusing to die a martyr's death, will have chosen to forfeit forever their eternal life with Father God in Heaven. This is a reality many will be facing during the times of tribulation.

Here we come to see how the Baptism of the Holy Spirit and Fire (The Promise of the Father) is given, to help us overcome areas where we are spiritually lacking and needing power and wisdom. The Promise of the Father gives us ability, by the power and leading of the Holy Spirit, to know the path we must take to dwell <u>within</u> the Kingdom of God. (It dwells within us; we need to learn how to dwell within it)! This is how the Apostles along with the 109 others, overcame their physical fear of torture and death; when on the day of Pentecost the Promise of the Father came upon them.

What about unconditional forgiveness toward others? Tell me, are there not some heinous offenses and crimes where we find it impossible to forgive? Yes, while under the influence of our uncrucified flesh, this often is the case. Here the mighty power of the Fire of Jesus' kind of Love (which accompanies the Baptism of the Holy Spirit) is required. With it, we may choose to please our Father in Heaven, by forgiving others their offenses, as He forgives ours. Is this not part of what Jesus prayed we would choose doing, as He taught the Our Father?

Yet in spite of this, some false teachers preach that God being all loving has forgiveness, which flows without any strings attached. What about Jesus' warning regarding what we must do before starting to pray, that our prayers may be heard and answered by our Father in Heaven? Did He not teach that before we even attempt to pray, if we have unforgiveness in our heart toward another, we must first go and find them, and ask their forgiveness of our unforgiveness? Why did Jesus say we must do this first? So that when we pray, our Father may forgive us of our offenses against Him, and be free to answer our prayers with blessings upon His obedient servants.

This all sounds good, but really aren't there some offenses so abhorrent we need not, nor are able to forgive? Again, you are speaking from uncrucified flesh. Perhaps one of the best examples of forgiveness, using the power of the Fire of Jesus' kind of Love, was given by the late Corrie Ten Boom. Fortunately, I was able to witness what she had to say on this issue, several years ago while being interviewed by Jim Bakker on the PTL Club.

Ms. Ten Boom said, having become a world traveling evangelist, after one meeting she conducted in Germany, a message was brought, regarding someone desiring to meet with her, who was seeking her forgiveness. Immediately she recognized the name on the note. Horror rose up inside, along with intense anger! The name was that of the German prison guard whom she had seen torture and kill her mother and father, along with her little sister.

"LORD, I CANNOT FORGIVE THIS MAN! PLEASE DO NOT ASK THIS OF ME!" Corrie prayed with all of her heart. Then by ministering of the Holy Spirit, the Fire of Jesus' love arose within saying, "Yes you can, and you **must forgive!**" She knew the Holy Spirit is the Spirit of Truth, and what He had spoken was God's will for her life.

At this moment of decision, Corrie used the Fire of Jesus' Love to pray, "Lord, although I in my flesh cannot forgive this man. In Your Spirit and by Your Love, You forgive him through me." Corrie then said to her assistant, "Let the man come in. I will meet with him." Seeing this man for the first time in many years, Corrie found the cold, hard look of evil was no longer on his countenance. He had a look of gentleness and kindness in his eyes, which were filled with tears.

✝ ✝ ✝ ✝

Crying as he spoke, this guard who had done so much evil to so many in the concentration camp, told Corrie of why he had needed to see her. He said he had become a born-again Christian. Having heard she was in town holding a crusade, he felt compelled to come see her, and ask forgiveness for what he had done to she and her family. He said he was begging her to forgive him, as the horror of what he had done was still within his mind. "Please forgive me. I did not know then what I was doing. I was under the influence of demons directing my life. I did not know Jesus as Lord of my life, as I do today"

Corrie looked upon this man with compassion, saying, "Through the power of Jesus' love, I forgive you." She said a great smile came upon the man's face, as he said a heavy burden (guilt and condemnation) had just been lifted from his spirit. Corry said that likewise, within her spirit, she felt release of a heavy weight (hatred, anger, and unforgiveness) which unaware, she had been carrying around for years. Both hugged and wept with joy, as great peace began to flood their spirits.

This is perhaps one of the best examples I know of, as to why it is important not only to seek the power of the Baptism of the Holy Spirit and Fire (The Promise of the Father); but also desire for it to consume the will of our sinful and lustful flesh. The true body and bride of Christ will be walking daily in this power. This is the only a bride worthy for Jesus returning for to claim as His Own.

WHAT IS THE PROMISE OF THE FATHER? IS THERE MORE?

The Promise of the Father is not necessarily a promise made to you and me. It originated in Father God having made a promise to Jesus, that He would honor the prayer Jesus prayed in behalf of His Bride. In the sincere prayer Jesus prayed to the Father in our behalf, He asked that His church, His Bride, would come together in love. Such a strong and real love, it would set her apart from every religion found in the world; love void of darkness and filled with Light.

Because of Jesus' prayer, Father God promised Him those members of the true body and bride of Christ, who were willing to reject religion, and seek the power to obey the 11th commandment given by Jesus, to **"love others, as I have loved you,"** should be able to receive the supernatural power to love unconditionally; thereby setting herself apart from every religion on earth.

In witnessing the power of **unity** in **unconditional love** (not <u>division</u> through pride in man made religious doctrines, dogmas, and traditions). Those in the world may no longer have any reason to doubt or be deceived by satan as to Who Jesus Is, by Whom He was sent, and Why. The Promise of the Father, will give us the means of <u>becoming</u> the true Bride of Christ; made up of powerful and faithful, "non religious" Christians!

The Promise of the Father is the answer to the "our Father," which Jesus taught us to pray. Manifestation of His Kingdom shall have come to all flesh, and as His Holy Spirit is poured out upon all flesh, His Will shall be done on earth just as it is in Heaven!

Lastly, the Promise of the Father shall be found in Father God's having furnished us with His Shekinah Glory! According to Jewish tradition, it is the Father of the bride who would furnish the wedding gown for the invited guests to wear, as well as the bride's gown. So it is as our Father gives to the Bride of Christ (Believers, who sought spiritual maturity in their faith, and received the Baptism of the Holy Spirit and Fire, then followed through in asking their life be used for the honor and glory of God) the Wedding garment fit for the Bride worthy of receiving Jesus, her Groom; a Bride which loves on the same level as Jesus.

When you begin to see this kind of Glory in the lives of those professing to be **believers**, you clearly will be able to discern the **<u>true</u> body and bride of Christ** from the false body and bride of man's empty and powerless "religion." When you see this Bride walking daily in **Unconditional Love**, winning spirits into the Kingdom of God – regardless the cost, helping them also to receive the Baptism of the Holy Spirit and Fire; then **look up, for your redemption draws near!**

CHAPTER ELEVEN
WHAT LOVING LIKE JESUS IS
AND IS NOT

For decades the teaching I had received said: Agape' (God's kind of Love) Love is Unconditional! This certainly sounds like our God. One morning while awakening I received a very important understanding from the Holy Spirit which added a caveat to that definition. We know from scripture "While we were yet sinners, God sent His only Son to suffer and die for us." By this, we are told of how God had first made manifest His Love for us. God still loved us, even when we in our rebellious and sinful nature were doing anything and everything but – loving Him.

All of this makes sense, especially when you get to know God personally through receiving Jesus as your Savior; and by the Holy Spirit receive enlightenment (quickening) of God's Word, which opens our spiritual eyes and ears. Knowing God personally we understand the description of the foundation of His nature – GOD IS LOVE!

Therefore it was shocking to me when the Holy Spirit revealed there is an important condition required to receive Jesus. Likewise, there is a serious condition which applies to all who choose to die in their sin, never asking Jesus to be their Lord and Savior. This sounds as if it is in conflict with "unconditional" love. We know that when we are forgiven, God throws our past sins into the sea of forgetfulness. Also any new sin committed may be placed under the Blood of Jesus and it too will be thrown away.

✟ ✟ ✟ ✟

The Holy Spirit choose to give me clarification as He pointed out the condition necessary to receive the power of forgiveness through the blood of Jesus. The precious blood which flows from God's Agape' Love to all mankind. That one condition, concept, and vital ingredient of character needed to receive forgiveness through the blood is: SINCERITY.

It is impossible to con God into forgiveness! How do I know this is so? Read the Word - "God is not mocked." Those who in spirit ask for forgiveness with an insincere attitude, seeking no power over sin, intending to go on sinning, will discover the Savior cannot allow His blood to cover their sin. Why can't He allow this? Because His blood is too precious, for by it our soul is purchased. By His blood we are able to receive the power of a new life as we are made a new creation in Christ.

But to what spirit does His blood apply? To the spirit which when coming to the cross sincerely repented; the spirit which contemplated sins with deep sorrow, contemplating all Jesus endured to save the soul entrusted to its care, from the pits of Hell; the spirit which sought more than forgiveness, but power to overcome sin; the spirit thirsting to be born again by the Holy Spirit of God. These are the spirits upon whom the precious blood of Jesus is poured out.

Drawing from my own life, may I give an example of insincere repentance and its cost? When I was in the second grade a bully decided to take me on. Being a bully he possessed the common <u>quality</u> known as cowardice. This guy was hiding in the bushes about three feet above the sidewalk as I came walking by. It was after school and I was on my way to catch the bus home. Suddenly I heard a loud yell from behind me. Turning to look, he sprang down on me, knocking me on my back and to the ground. He immediately used his knees to pin down my arms.

Sitting on top, he started punching me in the face. I tried my best to toss him off, but his position was too perfect for me to gain enough leverage. As the beating progressed I began to say with disgust, "I give up!" His reply was, "No you don't!" As he continued his beating I began to cry saying, "I'm going to tell the nuns on you!" Falsely I had hoped that threat would cause him to stop. But to my dismay he kept hitting me in the face, saying each time, "No you won't!"

✞　✞　✞　✞

Stubbornness made me take a few more punches before I finally agreed with him – I would not tell anyone about this beating. About five or six more punches after I had agreed, he stopped and walked away, leaving me laying on the sidewalk, my lip and nose bleeding.

Needless to say, all night that incident haunted me. How had I lost this fight? What must I do about it? Arriving at my decision, I realized I only lost because he had sprung from a hidden place, gaining surprise and a position leaving me helpless. But what should I do about it? That was easy! I decided my coerced offer of surrender surely must have been insincere. I was determined that the next day, I was going to prove how deeply insincere my promise really was.

After school the next day, as he was walking exactly where I had the day before, someone else was hiding in the bush. I gave out with a yell as I jumped down on him. When he turned to face me, it was like déjà vu all over again – only I was on top, and beating <u>his</u> face. It only took about three or four punches until realizing the hopelessness of his situation, the bully began to cry saying, "Please don't hit me anymore, I give up!" When I hit him once more, his crying and screams became louder. "Please stop, you're hurting me! I give up!"

Never being one wanting to deliberately hurt someone seriously (unless it became necessary) even in combat, I got off of him. (Believe it or not, I used to pray for the bully's I had fought, asking of God that I had not caused any severe injury, only that I had taught them not to desire to be a bully).

This bully did not offer to thank me for my act of kindness. I walked over to pick up my books, and as I was bending down a rock flew past my head just missing. When I looked at him, realizing the rock had missed its mark, he froze in fear. As I began running toward him, he at first just stood there in fear. When he finally started to run I made a perfect tackle and immediately was on top of him again, pinning him down.

This time even before I landed my first punch, he was eager to seek my forgiveness. Crying real tears, he was saying, "I'm sorry! Please forgive me!" To which I replied, "No you're not!" and "No I won't!" It did not take too many punches as I continued ignoring his repentance, until he began to change his remarks. "I'm going to tell the nuns on you" he began to say. I was thinking where have I heard that before? Remembering only yesterday, it was me, I continued punching him in the face. With each punch saying, "No you're not!"

It did not take him receiving as many punches as had I, until he emphatically agreed, he would tell no one! Giving him a few more punches after his agreement not to tell. I said, "I just want to make sure this time you're sincere – no more lies!" Each spoken word of my sentence was accompanied by a punch to the face. He gave me very deep and sincere assurance that he was indeed not lying, and would never ever again even think of fighting me.

His depth of sincerity moved me to let him up, although he just seemed to want to lay there bleeding, much as I had done the day before. You would think this story had a happy conclusion. But wait! Who said bully's have a working brain? Only a week later I had to take on this guy and four of his friends. The story of that battle is one for the books! In fact, I'm including it in my autobiography.

The moral of that lengthy story is, insincerity can and does require consequences to be paid. This incident happened a long time ago. I was not born again, and now know I am commanded by Jesus to love others as He loves the church. I understand better today it was the demon in his heart he was listening to, which had caused him to be a cowardly bully in the first place. Had I known the weapons of my warfare are not carnal, but mighty through the Holy Spirit in tearing down strongholds of evil, I might have acted in a more loving way toward my brother's flesh, and in a very aggressive way toward the demon controlling his actions.

✞ ✞ ✞ ✞

Carlote, you said there is a condition we must avoid. Does not God reach out to even the coldest of sinners with His Love? Yes indeed He does! By constant conviction regarding the evil of sin; with which the Holy Spirit calls upon sinners to sincerely repent and ask Jesus into their heart, freely choosing to surrender all to Him. All souls are important to God. It is by His breath they are created. Yet there are those whose spirit has no concern regarding their soul (the breath of God) being sentenced to spend eternity in Hell.

This brings us to that other condition – the unpardonable sin which is – Blasphemy against the Holy Spirit. We are cautioned this among all sins is the one for which we can find no forgiveness. What a horrible thing to happen! Many are confused, as I was for decades, over just what this sin might be; afraid that out of ignorance somehow we could have committed such a sin, worrying about the fate awaiting us.

The Holy Spirit in giving me understanding took away the fear and misunderstandings I had about the nature of this unpardonable sin. Blasphemy against the Holy Spirit, what is it? It is making the choice of committing spiritual suicide. How? Saying no to every plea of the Holy Spirit to sincerely repent of sin, and receive new life through the blood of Jesus. Not just saying no, but saying **no** with your very last breath. At that point in time, Tilt! Game Over, time has ended. You must now face eternity, having run out of the opportunities and time you were given to reply sincerely to the Holy Spirit's conviction of sin in your life. For the last time, you said no to His plea for you with a repentant and sincere heart to receive Jesus as your Lord and Savior.

When time ends – eternity begins. Time ends: time for playing games with God's offer of salvation; time of allowing satan to deceive you into running away from God's love; time of proudly boasting to others about how you don't need a Savior. Time for boasting about how you have no fear of God, satan, or hell, is **gone**! GAME OVER – satan WON! YOU LOST!

The day in which your Eternity begins, spiritual eyes you chose to keep blinded by darkness, will be opened to the light. The spiritual ears which you had turned deaf at the sound of God's Holy Spirit pleading for you to repent - will be opened at last to hear. Yes sadly, your spiritual eyes will see the loss of eternal life in Heaven you must suffer, in having chosen to die in your sins. Your opened spiritual ears, will now hear only the judgment of a Holy God, as the wages of your sin are given for your soul to pay. Hearing, you will come to understand at last the truth. Truth which hearing so many times you rejected. **"THE WAGES OF SIN IS (ETERNAL AND SPIRITUAL) DEATH. BUT THE GIFT OF GOD IS ETERNAL (AND SPIRITUAL) LIFE, THROUGH JESUS CHRIST (Messiah) – HIS SON."**

We are living in the "last days," a time in which God has promised to pour out His Holy Spirit upon all flesh. Please get on board – don't miss the boat! The cost of your ticket is simply a sincere repentant heart, and a hunger to know, love, and serve your Lord and Heavenly Father.

Sincere repentance is a cost you cannot afford not to pay. It is the price you must not refuse paying. Sincerity of heart, a hunger in your soul and spirit for your relationship with your Heavenly Father to be restored; just compare it to the price our Savior paid for your soul and mine. He paid the price we owe for our sin. Can we not pay the price we owe for our salvation – SINCERE REPENTANCE?

If you are finding these words bringing conviction to your heart, it is the voice of the Holy Spirit calling you to sincere repentance. Please surrender the eternal destination of your soul and spirit to the Love of God made manifest for you and me – Jesus, the Savior of the world.

✝ ✝ ✝ ✝

Along with the Holy Spirit I plead with you, please do not choose to miss this opportunity! You never know just when you might be hearing your last call to repentance. But even more, each day without Jesus, you are missing opportunities to store up treasure in Heaven. Will you unwisely choose to be among the poorest of souls living in Heaven; having produced no fruit of spiritual value in your life here on earth?

This decision rests entirely with you. God never forces any to accept His gift of Redemption and Love through His Son Jesus. He only presents Him to you with Love, through His Word and by the conviction of His Spirit. If you are one living in unrepentant sin, and are still reading this book, not yet having put it down to go to God in prayer, may I ask you to once more consider the consequences? Now is the time of salvation! Now is the time to seek your spiritual eyes and ears to be open by the Spirit of Truth! Now is the time to cast satan and his demons out of you life! Right now, it is time for you to seek to become born again, by the Spirit of God!

Are you willing to do this? If so, please put down this book (its pages will be waiting for you when you return), and go to Jesus with a sincerely repentant heart. Seek the new life and power He desires to give you. Don't worry about saying some fancy prayer, one with all of the "right" words. The "right" words will flow from the sincerity in your heart, as you surrender all to Jesus.

CHAPTER TWELVE
"AND YOU SHALL RECEIVE POWER"

"And you shall receive Power, after the Holy Spirit is come upon you; and you shall be witnesses of Me in Judea, Jerusalem, Samaria, and to the uttermost places of the earth." In our fleshly mind we think of the word power, and immediately refer to the idea of mental or physical strength, but this is not what Jesus was referring to. He was speaking of Spiritual Power. That which is born of the flesh is flesh; that which is born of the Spirit (of God) is Spiritual.

To understand what Jesus was truly telling us we must close the eyes of our flesh to open those of our spirit, seeing through the Holy Spirit Who resides within. In doing so we must ask ourselves, what is the greatest power in all of Heaven and earth? The answer is easy. It is what God's personality is made of – LOVE! The power Jesus was referring to, is the kind of power Adam and Eve were tricked into believing they could attain by partaking of the forbidden fruit in the Garden of Eden: the power to be like God.

The power Jesus offers is the ability to be able to give His kind of Love to others. It is the Promise of the Father come to pass, that we may receive the power to love unconditionally, while living here on earth. It is the same kind of Love which exists in Heaven. With this in mind, we can see Jesus was not referring to becoming born again <u>by</u> the Spirit of God, but receiving the Power contained <u>within</u> the Baptism of the Holy Spirit and **Fire**.

Would you like proof of what I just said? When Jesus first appeared to the Apostles, before departing we are told He breathed upon them saying: **"Receive you the Holy Spirit."** At that very instant in time, each Apostle present became born again <u>by</u> the Spirit of God. They had within the Spirit of Truth, Who would reveal Truth to them, leading and guiding them to walk faithfully in the Truth, teaching it to others.

But after this infilling of the Spirit of Truth came to them from Jesus Himself, did they run into the streets and start preaching the Gospel (The Good News – the Kingdom of God is at hand) to everyone they came into contact with? We know the answer to that is no, but why not? Because in their flesh they were still a scared bunch of chickens! In their flesh they feared what kind of torture and death they might encounter if they dared tell even one person about Jesus, the Messiah, and God's plan of redemption which in Him is fulfilled. They loved their flesh and greatly feared for its safety more than they loved others. They possessed no concern or fear regarding the eternal destination of their brothers and sisters immortal souls.

Even though they had become born again by the Spirit of God, it took something special, a profound <u>Spiritual</u> <u>Power</u>, for the Apostles to overcome such fleshly fear. It took the ability of being able to keep the eleventh commandment issued by Jesus. "<u>Love</u> <u>others</u>, **the <u>same</u> <u>way</u> I have <u>loved</u> you**." Without the promised gift of the Father, the Baptism by Jesus Himself, of the Holy Spirit and Fire; the church He established would never have started. The <u>Power</u> of **Perfect Love cast out fear!**

This is exactly what happened not only to the Apostles, but to the others gathered with them in the upper room. "Suddenly there came a sound as of a mighty rushing wind" This was the mighty infilling of the Holy Spirit. This time He was bringing with Him spiritual gifts of power to be given each according to how it pleased God. To one the gift of speaking in tongues, to another the gift of interpretation of what was said in tongues, to yet another gift of prophecy, and so on. Some received more than one gift, while others just one. Father God knew what each would do with the gift or gifts they received, in using them for His honor and glory.

We are told next, there came cloven tongues as of Fire, which settled over the head of each one assembled there. This was the Fire of Jesus' kind of Love – Agape, Unconditional and Perfect Love filling their spirit (will), driving away every fear, depositing a burning love toward the souls of their brothers and sisters who were spiritually starving, walking in darkness, and yearning to be set free from the law of sin and death.

It was the infilling Power of this kind of Love (Godly Love, the MOST POWERFUL force in both Heaven and earth), which <u>compelled</u> them to go out and preach the Gospel without any fear of what might happen to their mortal body. Starving souls must be fed, spirits walking in sin must be informed of God's plan of salvation, the Blood of Jesus, offering freedom from the shame, guilt, and bondage of sin!

We are informed that each of those 120 who faithfully gathered in the upper room had remained in one accord. They were not arguing over religious ideas of just what the "promise" of the Father might be. As the result, each was rewarded for obedience. All received the power and ability to keep the 11th commandment, to love others the same way in which Jesus Loves us.

Do we need such power in the church today? Has it not been "missing in action" for far too long? Did Father God forbid Jesus from Baptizing any more than those 120? Does not the promise of the Father extend to those of us living today? You need only to look at the twelve Ephesian men Paul ran across. When he laid his hands on them, did not each one receive the Baptism of Holy Spirit and Fire? This came from Jesus Himself, not St. Paul; he was only the conduit Jesus used.

I submit to you, not only is such power available to the True Body and Bride of Christ; it is needed badly in order to become the harvester of souls God intends all of us to be. We need this great Power, especially in these last days! Tell me, why is it among those born again of the Spirit of God, they allow fear of the pain of rejection to keep their mouth closed tight, when the Holy Spirit would have them be a strong witness of Jesus to others? They are lacking the ability and power of loving others, the same as Jesus loves them.

✟ ✟ ✟ ✟

Have you ever wondered why powerless fear is able of making one possessing the Spirit of Truth believe they are powerless and ineffective in their ability to be a witness of Jesus to others? (They are believers – but the wrong kind of believers. Believers in fear, through swallowing satan's lies, rather than believers possessing Faith, who were taught to know who they are in Jesus, and how to put on the mind of Christ)! Religion cannot and does not teach such things.

Jesus told us Himself just why this is. "You shall receive Power, **after** the Holy Spirit is come upon you; and you shall become witnesses of Me... to the uttermost parts of the earth." The answer is simply too much Religion is being taught by <u>man.</u> Sadly, not enough about the Power of the Loving Relationship with our Father (which Jesus came to restore to purity) is allowed to be taught by the **Spirit of Truth!**

So many Christian "Religions," filled with man's feeble and corrupt understanding of Scripture. Dogmas, doctrines and traditions of pride and division are being taught by those not possessing the Spirit of Truth. As a cover up for not asking or allowing the Holy Spirit to feed God's sheep, they teach the ability of possessing the Holy Spirit died with the last Apostle, along with spiritual gifts which bring honor and glory to God. What a pack of lies! Do you see how "Religion" has been used by satan to corrupt the teaching of the truth found in God's Word? To know the truth, and have the ability of understanding the spiritual food and drink it has for our spirit, we must not only be born again; but we must seek and gain the Baptism of the Holy Spirit and Fire, using the gift of discernment, to not permit satan's twisting of Scriptures, diluting the Word of God (as many of today's new translations of the Bible attempt doing).

✥ ✥ ✥ ✥

Far too many religious Churches are filled with teachers offering only John's baptism of repentance, never once offering to teach how we may seek receiving personally from Jesus, His Baptism of the Holy Spirit and Fire. Many are members of churches who are satisfied with having had their ears tickled by hearing: "You MUST be born again!" They happily get dunked in water; and as my Pastor says: some go in a dry sinner, and come up a wet sinner; going through the motions, without true heartfelt surrender to Jesus of <u>Everything</u> in their life. So many never are being taught that becoming born again is only the <u>beginning</u> of attaining powerful spiritual gifts which our Heavenly Father desires to bestow on us.

Such Christians, like the Pharisee who looked down on the Publican, go around with self-righteous pride thinking of others: "I'm born again, and you're not! La, la la," while the sinner says in their heart to God, "Lord, have mercy on me, a sinner." Just as bad, are those who flaunt the gift of being able to speak in tongues, babbling in front of one not possessing this gift, as if wanting to say: "Look what I can do, and you can't!"

ABUSE of this wonderful gift, is NOT what God has in mind. In fact, He gave us teaching from St. Paul as to how we are to use this gift of a Heavenly language. It is for the edification (uplifting) of the church, or the edification of ourselves, as the Holy Spirit makes utterance to the Father in our behalf; telling Him of things we have need of, which we are unaware.

Let's look at the first purpose, edifying the church. Saint Paul cautioned, if one were to speak out loud in church, let it be <u>ONLY</u> if there is another present having the gift of interpreting what has been said. But how do you know if an interpreter is present? Simple, just let God's Will (The Holy Spirit) and not the will of your flesh, direct the opening and speaking out loud of your mouth. Those desiring to show off their gift to others, care less about what Paul taught or why he taught as he did. They are going to open their big mouth, regardless of how many others may have given a message!

This brings us to another teaching of Paul about speaking out loud in tongues while in church. Let it be by no more than <u>three</u>! I asked the Holy Spirit why only three? He said the church may receive a message from God the Father, God the Son, and God the Holy Spirit. But there is no god the blabbermouth! Far too many times I have witnessed services where four, five, six, seven or even more people have uttered "messages" from God (?) in tongues.

No one being present to interpret even the first effort, obviously this was not from God. Many times it is only people wishing to show off their gift, the poor Pastor is placed under the burden of interpreting what each of those seven, eight, or nine messages said. When interpreting the fourth on, those messages tend to become wearier and devoid of any spiritual value. Shame on such Pastors! Going along with the sham of pretending they have actually heard from God more than three messages; rather than correcting this misuse of the gift of speaking in tongues!

There is a more specific reasoning given by Paul as to why speaking out loud should be done only if there is one present who truly has the gift of interpretation, and why no more than three messages are ever truly given by God. It concerns the desire not to allow this gift to become a stumbling block to someone who is visiting for the first time. Sad is the way some Pastors chose to just blurt out in tongues while teaching; seeking to impress their listeners that the Holy Spirit is really "inspiring" the message they are giving.

St. Paul states that new visitors, having no teaching regarding the gift of tongues will think, "These people are a bunch of crazies! I'm out of here, never to return again!" Pastor, church member, your abuse of this gift, using it for self aggrandizement, may have caused many to flee from your presence. Do you not care that on the Day of Judgment you must give to God accounting for such behavior? There is no power within the church when you choose abusing this gift from God, because there is no Love motivating your use, it is self-edifying only, and not for the edification of the church, as God intends.

Am I saying tongues should not be spoken out loud in church? Some will try to twist the truth to make such a claim. But the facts speak for their self. I will give you a perfect example of the proper use of speaking in tongues "out loud" while in church. In 1974 after having become born again, I attended service at Christian Retreat in Bradenton Florida. This was my first time inside of <u>any</u> church in over two years, as I had been seeking truth, and finding only man's bigoted and powerless religious teachings available. The Holy Spirit had directed me to attend Christian Retreat, which was a thirty mile drive from my home in St. Petersburg.

The praise & worship service at the start was Awesome! Then Pastor Gerald Derstine, the man I had watched several times on television, with a program called Kingdom Living, came to the pulpit and began to speak. Barely had he started speaking, when all of a sudden a man across the aisle from me popped up and began to jabber in an unknown tongue – <u>out</u> <u>loud</u>, with the emphasis on the word LOUD! Oddly enough, no one made any effort to stop him or escort him out the door.

Coming from a Catholic background, naturally this puzzled me. Had I been sitting next to him, I would have offered to show him they way to the door. This guy's disrupting the service by not allowing Gerald to continue speaking. Why are they allowing this obvious nut case to go on doing this? These were my immediate thoughts. But then he did stop, and sat back down in his seat. You won't believe what happened next! A little old lady sitting next to me (she looked like she might have been in her 90's) stood up, and began speaking out loud in English. What she said was so beautiful and sincere. I could hardly believe my ears!

After she finished there was a time of silence (they were waiting to see if God had any more messages to give). Then Pastor Gerald began to once more speak from the pulpit. He said: "For benefit of those of you who might be new here, please let me explain what has just occurred." He went on to tell about this gift of speaking in tongues, and how God intends that it be used for the edification of His church. He told of how the man had been instructed by the Holy Spirit to speak boldly out loud, because God had a message for the church this day. He also said that this was not an everyday occurrence, but happened only when God had something to say to His church.

Gerald then went on to tell of how the lovely lady had been used by God to interpret His message in English so all may understand what it consists of. I knew this sounded right, as what the lady had spoken was one of the most powerful and beautiful prayers for the church I had ever heard in my life. Besides, Gerald had pointed out to us, just where this is found in the Bible. He read Scriptures relating to the gift of speaking in tongues, as we followed along in our Bibles. Having been raised Catholic I knew very little about what the Bible had to say, or what spiritual gifts, if any, Father God desired to impart in order to help in my growth, as I worked toward attaining maturity.

"WE" (Catholics), relied mainly on teachings contained in the Catechism, the mighty word of **man**! This was why if any ever asked: "Are you a "Christian"? Our proud response would be: "No, I'm a **Catholic**!" Further, should they inquire as to if we knew where our Bible was. We would calmly and assuredly say, "Sure, I think the last place I saw it was on the coffee table in the living room, sitting under twelve years of dust."

If this offends any "Religious" person, please understand. It is the truth being revealed out of love. I once lived there, under such powerless religious bondage and oppression of laws and rituals created by man, not God. Until the wonderful day when Jesus set me free, and gave me His Holy Spirit, the Spirit of Truth, to dwell inside, and lead me into all truth. The very One Who inspired the writing of God's Word now lives within! When I ask and permit Him to, He reveals Truth from God's Word which helps feed my spirit the Bread of life, and brings Living Water to my parched soul. The Holy Spirit by the Word of God guides me each day in choosing to walk on the path of righteousness. This helps me live an abundant life filled with heavenly peace and a joy you cannot find the words to express. I may even bring forth His Fruit in my life for the honor and glory of my Heavenly Father.

This teaching regarding speaking in tongues, which I have so boldly proclaimed by the Holy Spirit, will be called by those wishing to continue abusing this great gift from God, words of condemnation. Those who in pride reject what is spoken of here, in pride believe "my way" is the ONLY way; they will boldly say, "God knows my heart!" To which I reply, indeed He does! This is why He, from His heart, has offered to send you correction in these matters!

But the Holy Spirit has revealed to me that I will be called a false teacher, by those who are **false teachers**. What I have taught is not from words of condemnation, as the father of lies would have you believe. They are of edification and correction, and are not of my ideas, but come from the teachings the Holy Spirit gave to St. Paul, way before me. Had I not been able to back up by the Word of God my teaching concerning the abuse of this gift, then surely the term false teacher would apply. But the wise among you will heed and apply the proper response to this teaching.

Still, for many Pastors choosing to spout out blips of tongues while teaching, simply to impress their listeners; and/or encourage their members to "stretch forth their hands and everyone **pray in tongues**;" it will be as if I had thrown stones at a hornet's nest. Of course I never got to actually hear St. Paul, mighty man of God, as he preached or taught a crowd of people. But I am certain if he ever stopped to speak words in tongues, it was only because God had a powerful and relevant message for the church to hear. I am also certain he would not have been the one interpreting every time such a thing was to occur. He would wait and listen, as another gave the interpretation. Then all would know this is of God.

I believe when St. Paul was preaching or teaching the Gospel, he did so in a language all could clearly understand. Did he not say he would prefer to speak just ten words which all could understand, than ten thousand words in tongues? Clearly, Saint Paul was not one to "show off" this precious gift from God. I also believe whenever he prayed in tongues for his own benefit it was alone, between he and God. So if you feel you have a problem with Carlote of Florida, let me tell you it is more of a problem with Paul of Tarsus. Although I cannot speak for Paul of Tarsus, I believe he would refer you to take your problem to the Holy Spirit; telling Him you do not like His repression on the gift you have been given. See just how far you get with that!

If you are a Pastor or church member who has been abusing and misusing the gift of speaking in tongues out loud in church. Not for edification of the church, but rather yourself. I ask by the Holy Spirit, that you make the choice to quit doing it! It's really that simple. The message offered is: if you are guilty - the Holy Spirit will reveal this to you, repent and change your ways.

Why is this so important? Because the True Body and Bride of Christ is about to arise in Power and Glory! She will be in ONE ACCORD! This means having no man-made doctrines, dogmas, and traditions to separate her by the stain of religion or wrinkle of schism on her wedding gown! She will be Radiant with the Truth and abounding in Agape' Love toward all. She will be found daily walking in the Power of the Baptism of the Holy Spirit and Fire!

There shall be an abundance of bold and mighty warriors in the One True God's Army of Love, Life, and Light; using the Sword of the Spirit with power against demons in the life of others. Yet the Bride will possess a humbleness of spirit, because the Fire of Jesus' kind of Love will make of her great harvesters among those in the world.

The True Body and Bride of Christ will not be full of herself, pride fully abusing spiritual gifts. She will be dead to self, humbly full of the Holy Spirit's guidance, that such gifts might bring edification to the church, and honor and glory to the One True God! In other words, she will not be RELIGIOUS!

What demon can stand against the Sword of the Spirit? What human heart can resist the power of the kind of Love Jesus has? What kind of person wishing to call themselves "Christian" would in pride, reject this calling from the Spirit of God? Will the choice of your free will be to continue waking in powerless Religion, being governed by the laws, demands, and regulations of man? Or will you yield to only the guidance of God's Holy Spirit, as you pursue knowing and living to the fullest, in the kind of Loving Relationship Father God desires you to know and share not only with Him, but with your brothers and sisters as well?

God never interferes with our free will, which is our spirit He gave this free will to you and me as part of making us in His image. We know from Jesus our spirit is willing, but our flesh is weak. For this reason, God offers to us the guidance of His Holy Spirit (His Will). But He never forces us to seek or accept His guidance. We must first choose to die to self, yielding our spirit (will) to that of God's Will (His Holy Spirit). Jesus set the example for us when in the Garden of Gethsemane, He proclaimed to the Father: "Not My will, but Yours be done!" If we truly love God, and seek to walk within His Kingdom, this will be our prayer at the start of each day.

In the end it all comes down to faith. What are you placing your faith in? Is it the powerless religion of man, which does not teach about or permit you to grow spiritually strong through receiving from Jesus, the Baptism of the Holy Spirit and Fire? Or is it in the Powerful and Loving relationship you share daily in with your Father in Heaven, through the forgiveness and restored relationship provided by the blood of His Son, and by the leading of the Spirit of Truth? Remember Jesus has made it clear that upon His arrival, He will be looking to find FAITH alive and well within the hearts of those calling themselves "Christian." But as always, faith in the religious, powerless teachings of man, which produces little or no works, is **dead**.

Let your Faith be alive! Walking, talking, and living daily in the Kingdom of God, leading others to join you in dwelling there! Daily feeding upon God's Word, that you may put on the whole armor of God, and go into battle skillfully using the mighty Sword of the Spirit! These (Fierce Soldiers in the Army of the One TRUE God), are those whom Jesus will call to meet Him in the clouds!

CHAPTER THIRTEEN
THE IMPORTANCE OF THE "FIRE"

We often think there are only Ten Commandments, and have difficulty keeping them. However, little or no thought is given to keeping the eleventh commandment. The commandment Jesus Himself gave us: **"A new commandment I give unto you; that you love one another <u>as I have loved you,</u> that you also love one another."** (John, 13:34) .We know all the law and all the prophets are fulfilled by obeying only the first two commandments; both of which deal with love. (Matt. 22:40) But the first two commandments were given in the Old Testament days, a time in which the Light of Life was still withdrawn from man. The eleventh commandment was given by Jesus to those in whom the Light of Life has been restored.

Just think what would happen if every Christian in the Body of Christ were to truly love one another <u>as Jesus loves us</u>? What would happen to the kingdom of darkness, if we who are capable, took Jesus' kind of love to the hearts of those in bondage to satan? This includes our relatives, friends, neighbors, those we work with, and also our worst of enemies. If we were to share the love of God abroad in our heart with those in foreign lands - how could satan find recruits for terrorist?

To most Christians today this sounds like a fantasy, an "unrealistic" good idea, which never can happen. But just stop and ask yourself, would Jesus command us to do something and not offer us the ability to gain the power needed to do it? We know from God's Word, without Him we can do nothing; but with Him **ALL** things are possible. I believe the main reason for the eleventh commandment receiving so little reverence in our daily walk, is because as of yet, no one by the influence of the Holy Spirit, has instructed the soldiers in God's Army as to how we may become able (attain the power) to love as Jesus loves. This information is vital for the True Body and Bride of Christ to know!

☨ ☨ ☨ ☨

Jesus' kind of love has no empty words and artificial embraces. His love does not seek "what can I get from you;" but rather, "what can I give to you to enrich your faith, peace, and joy." Jesus' love has no room for hatred, anger, religious or racial bigotry! Jesus' kind of love brings Light, Life, Freedom, Peace, and Joy to all who are embraced by it. I have no long list of scriptures to back up what I have just stated. But all who have encountered the reality of Jesus' love know beyond any doubt, that all I have stated and even more are true.

So how can we ever learn to give Love to others on the "unconditional forgiving" level? The answer is very simple; as I stated in the pervious chapter. Seek and allow Jesus to Ignite The Fire which accompanies the Baptism of the Holy Spirit (Luke, 3:16). Jesus is the one Baptizing us with the Holy Spirit and Fire. The FIRE is the same kind of Love which Jesus has for us. More than just allow, we should diligently ask of Jesus to fan the FIRE with the Wind of the Holy Spirit. We ask, in our prayers at the start of each new day, and by our seriously studying the Word of God under the influence of the Holy Spirit.

The Baptism of the Holy Spirit gives us the capability of doing mighty works for the Kingdom of God. But if we were to do so without the Fire as our motive, such works are all in vain. Here's an example of what I've just said. There are those who <u>work</u> at producing works such as casting out demons, and healing the sick. However, their motive is to be able to tell God on the day of Judgment, "You <u>Owe</u> <u>Me</u> a Huge Mansion for all of the Works I have done in Your name!" We already know what God's reply to them will be: **"Depart from Me, you workers of iniquity, I <u>Never</u> <u>Knew</u> <u>You</u>!"** (Matthew, 7:23)

✠ ✠ ✠ ✠

No <u>work</u> is involved producing spiritual works, when motivated by the Fire of Jesus' kind of Love. The Fire gives us a purity of purpose which brings honor and glory to our Father and an answer to the prayer Jesus prayed for us to His Father, by being in one accord with our brothers and sisters in the unity of love. St. Paul spoke of the "Fire," in 1st Corinthians chapter 13, verses 1-3. He warns of works which are lacking Love as their motive. Why is the "Fire" so important? As Paul said in vs. 3 doing all of these seemingly Godly things without the motive of love, <u>it</u> <u>profits</u> <u>us</u> **NOTHING!**

This brings us to the best tasting meat of God's Word. We are warned that on the Day of Judgment, the foundation (motive) of our works shall be tried by Fire. This is a trial no one shall avoid (not even the "saved"), for everyone's works will be tried by the Fire. Each will receive their reward based on what remains after being tested by the "Fire." It is the "Fire" which gives us the drive or ability, to do that which we are capable of doing; and that is produce spiritual works for the Kingdom of God. There are different kinds of spiritual works, none of which will perish: those of **Gold**, motivated by our love for God; those of **Silver**, motivated by our love for our neighbor as our self; and finally works of **Precious Stones**, which are motivated by (unconditionally) loving others, just as Jesus loves us. In each of these works, the common motivator is Love.

The message God has given me is simple, yet profound! The "Fire" we are given with the Baptism of the Holy Spirit, is the <u>same</u> **Fire** which will try our works. The other name for this Fire, is Godly Love, the same Love with which Jesus Loves us. When tried by Love, works we have done out of selfish motives (wood) will perish; works we have done to manipulate and use others (hay) will perish. Likewise, works done to reap ill gotten gain (such as lying to make a sale = stubble), will perish when tried by Love.

✚   ✚   ✚   ✚

But the "Fire of Love" will permit works motivated by the "Fire of Love" to pass safely through. **Works of Gold, Silver, and Precious Stones, have eternal value - they will last forever!** Such works are part of the Kingdom of God here on earth, and belong eternally to the Kingdom of Heaven, where only Love prevails. Doing these works is our way of showing gratitude to Jesus for having Baptized us with the Holy Spirit. By doing these works we bring honor and glory to our Father. **"Herein is My Father glorified, that you bear much fruit; so shall you be My disciples."** (John, 15:8) Doing works motivated by loving others as Jesus loves us (unconditionally), is the fulfillment of the eleventh commandment. Our Lord Jesus told us clearly: "If you love Me. Keep My commandments."

It is so important for us to put the "Fire" of Jesus' kind of Love on the front burner of our life and set the Flame to High. Far too many of us become so distracted by our busy life, we tend to place the Fire on the back burner and put the Flame on <u>Low</u>. This is what I had done, until one day the Holy Spirit revealed to me I was on my way to being among the poorest of souls living eternally in Heaven. That was all the motivation I needed to become serious in pursuing the "Fire" in my life. I have come now to realize how important Love is to every aspect of my life. Not just loving those who love me, but also loving those who hate me, loving those walking in darkness, this includes "terrorists"

I pray constantly that the Love of Jesus will save them from following after death and darkness. Jesus' Love is the **only** realistic way of ending terrorism. His Love must be seen by those in darkness, revealed in the lifestyle of we who have received from Jesus the Baptism of the Holy Spirit and Fire!

Basically it involves loving all who need to see the Love of Jesus being manifest in my life that they may be ministered to by Jesus' Love. Who needs to see the Love of Jesus? <u>Everyone</u>! To whom should we desire to show the Love of Jesus to? <u>Everyone</u>! Jesus' kind of Love is the answer to everyone's needs. The Love of Jesus is the cure for every immoral disease satan is trying to spread throughout the world. GOD IS LOVE! He gives to us, His redeemed sons and daughters, the ability to share His Love with others; through following the guidance of the Holy Spirit. How can we say **no** to Him? Yet so often that is what we say, every time we choose to produce only works of wood, hay, and stubble. Jesus said that to be His follower, we must daily pick up our cross. Choosing to pick up our cross means we are willing to make a sacrifice of love. We have the free will to walk away, leaving the cross lying for another day. But God's Word tells us <u>each day</u>, we must decide what we will do regarding the cross set before us. Our lazy flesh will tell us the cross is too heavy a burden to bear. But if we listen, the Holy Spirit will tell us, herein is your Father glorified, and herein is your eternal reward. Which voice we chose to listen to and follow will be brought to Light when the works we did are tried by Fire on the Day of Judgment.

The prayer of our Savior to His Father before going to suffer and die on the cross needs to be answered. Jesus prayed that we would become "ONE" body of believers, united by LOVE. The body divided by man made doctrines, dogmas, and religious bigotry is not a Bride **worthy** of Jesus returning for. A church looked upon as just another of the world's many confused "religions," (because of rampant label worship and religious bigotry) is not one desirous of being what Jesus asked His Father for us to be. Jesus prayed for us to be able to achieve results. He said the reason for His prayer was so those in the world would come to fully understand; **Who He Is** - The SAVIOR of the world, **By Whom He Was Sent** - Our Heavenly Father, Who Loves us so much, and **Why HE Made The Sacrifice Of Love On The Cross** - to restore our position as the "Redeemed" sons and daughters of God!

We all need the Fire of Jesus' Love burning strong and alive within our spirit! The world in which we live is very cold and getting colder. Many hearts are full of "religion," and therefore in bondage to satan's guidance, having no knowledge of God's Love, and the relationship Jesus came to restore for them. satan has closed their heart to human love; this is how Moslems are able to so easily find "suicide bombers" and practice barbaric works of evil. Only the "Fire" of Jesus' Love can overpower and melt the heart frozen by hatred. Only the Light of Jesus' Love can drive away the ugly darkness which destroys hope in the spirit. Only Jesus' kind of Love can convict the coldest and hardest of hearts to repent of allowing a stupid jerk like satan to guide their heart.

We must diligently seek after, and let the Fire of Love motivate our words and actions! Those who do this will become the **Glorious** and **Beautiful Bride of Christ**! **Then Christians will become looked upon as people who walk in Righteousness, Love, Peace, and Joy. A Christian is one not possessing religion, but a relationship with the One True and Living God. We are able to worship God in spirit and in truth, not with empty hearts and "religious words." We will not be busy trying to show other's how pious we are. We will be showing to our Father, through yielding to the guidance of the Holy Spirit, our desire to be Holy as our Father is Holy. I don't believe we can ever get enough of this wonderful gift of "Fire" within our spirit.**

There may be some who fear receiving the "Fire," such as those who find being a pew warming label wearer is all the responsibility they want to have as a Christian. There may also be those who have done as I did, placed the Fire on the back burner, and set the flame on low. There are also those who cherish possessing the Fire, but just like me, they desire even more of the Fire within. God did not give me this teaching to share, only to leave us in that state of want. He wishes to satisfy our desire for the Fire of Jesus' Love to be alive in our spirit.

For those fearing the Fire of Jesus' Love invading their heart, it may be the hardest of decisions. As a Minister of God's Word I am very concerned over whom you submit to as master of your life, who you will choose listening to and obeying. Some fear surrendering to and receiving the Fire of God's Love, because of its power to change their life-style. The change may cost the loss of "friends" they like to hang out with. May I suggest you be more concerned with your immortal soul not being "lost," or being among the poorest in Heaven? How about being more concerned that your "friends" should not be "lost" to satan?

There is so much to gain and nothing of real value to be lost in seeking this Blessing which the Fire of Jesus' Love will give you. Not only will your soul not be lost through-out eternity. Also, your spirit will attain the power, desire, compassion, and ability to be a witness of the Kingdom of God within to others, even your worst of enemies. The FIRE will enable you to be labeled a Christian by others, because of the "Fruit" produced in your life. Not because of the religious label you like to brag about.

It is a cold, hard, and cruel world we are living in. Without the Fire of Jesus' love being made manifest in the life of His followers, it waxes colder every passing day. The only way we can travel through it safely and victoriously is in having the power of the Love of Jesus' alive within our heart. Any who would choose to embrace this world rather than the Love of Jesus, don't blame God or me. Blame sa-tan, the one whose voice you choose to listen to and obey. But know this, one day you may get tired of his deceptions, and of all the misery and sorrows he has caused your life to know. If you are still alive on that day, seek out a Spirit filled church, and seek to receive the blessing of becoming born again. Then once you have become a new creation and are born of the Spirit, ask Jesus to Baptize you with the Holy Spirit and Fire. If you have chosen to attend a Spirit filled church, there will always be someone alive with the Fire willing to pray for you to receive the power you need to live for God, know Him, recognize and obey His voice, and be used by Him to love others into His Kingdom.

Remember, regardless of how cold the world may become, the Fire of Jesus' love is all you and I need. It will help us endure life in this world, and to one day enter into Heaven with Joy. May God Bless and answer the request of all who hunger to receive this Blessing. I pray in Jesus name. Amen.

CHAPTER FOURTEEN
DOING GREATER WORKS
THAN JESUS DID!

Real Power! We as the redeemed sons and daughters of God should be excited about the Power we have within, rather than take it for granted. It is the power to reflect the image of the One, True, Living God of Love and Light, to those who do not know Him. Are you excited yet? We have within, the power to pray for the sick and watch them be healed in the name of Jesus. We may cast out demons sending them running back to Hell, again in the name of Jesus. This **Power** is given us as **believers**! We simply must choose to **believe**, **pray with Faith** and use the Fire of Jesus' Love, as we Love others just like Jesus Loves us.

To sum it up, we have the power to do for ourselves and for others, the same things Jesus did, making faith in God more than just a word, in both our life and the lives of others. Remember Saint Paul said, **"I spoke not with the enticing words of man, but with the demonstration of the Holy Spirit and power; that your faith may**

not be based upon man's wisdom, but the Power of God" (1 Corinthians, 2: 4 & 5).

Saint Paul did the same works which Jesus did, and even greater. Jesus told us as His disciples, we who **receive** His teachings with gladness, and **believe** with all of our heart (= followers, Christians, **Believers,** sons and daughters of God), would be able to not only do the works He did, but even **greater works** (John, 14:12). Have you ever wondered just what those **greater works** might be? I know I have often pondered this question. In fact, it is a question I have had for many years. It was not until now, as I was writing this chapter, the answer was revealed to me.

I have often worried that pride might have an opportunity to enter if we were to be thinking the works we did were **greater** than those of Jesus. But after the answer I received, I can see how in God's wisdom, we can indeed do **greater works**, and only God will receive the honor and glory. In fact, pride doesn't have a chance! I'm sure by now, every reader must be screaming at me saying "TELL ME!" O.K., I will!

✟   ✟   ✟   ✟

First, in doing the works Jesus did, I used to think we didn't have to suffer in our flesh, and die on the cross for the love of others. But the Holy Spirit has revealed to me that oh yes we do – and daily! When we choose each morning to deny our self, it's like placing a crown of thorns on our head, and lashing our flesh with a whip. When we then use the nails of righteousness, peace, and joy to crucify the will and lust of our flesh to the cross, our flesh is daily put to death.

We pick up our cross and follow Jesus when we make the choice to happily and willingly make a sacrifice of love; offering to give love to any needing to be loved. When Jesus is lifted up He draws all men unto Him (John, 12:32). Daily we must make the decision to die to self on the cross; that Jesus, through us, may reach others with His Love and reveal His work of salvation.

Let's look at the foundation we must have in order to make it possible for us to do the same works Jesus did. That foundation is Faith and Love! Not the kind of faith on a plaque which hangs on a wall in our room. It is Powerful and Living FAITH which is in the spirit and soul of one who is a **believer**. One who **believes,** has **no** doubt that the Word of God is **True**. We must learn how to know who we are in Christ and how to put on the mind of Christ. Neither is available to one lacking in faith, or whose faith wavers like a wave on the sea.

Jesus did not need the same kind of faith as we do. He did not have to **believe** God exists - He Is God! Jesus did not have to **believe** the Word of God is True. He **Is** the Living Word, Who was made flesh and came to dwell among us. Jesus did not have to learn Who He was in Christ - He was and is Christ, the "anointed one." The One anointed by the Father to become my Savior, your Savior, and the Savior of the world.

The only time in which Jesus had to put on the mind of Christ, was in the Garden of Gethsemane. It was there that the foul, caustic stench of your sins, my sins, and those of everyone who has or will live in this world, affected Jesus' fleshly spirit. That odor of sin from both the repentant and unrepentant began to overwhelm Jesus - Holy God. Because of this repugnant odor, and scenes of the tremendous pain and suffering which lay ahead, which satan was showing Jesus; His fleshly spirit began to agonize greatly, His body began sweating drops of blood. Then He passionately asked, **"Father, if it be possible, let this cup pass from Me!"** Immediately He was ministered to by the Holy Spirit, reminding Him of Who He Is. Putting on the mind of Christ, the promised Messiah then, in setting an example for us, said: **"Not My will Father, but Yours be done."**

Do you see how it requires **greater** effort for us to do the same kind of works which Jesus did? We are **not** God! But when our **great** **desire** is to **grow** in spiritual maturity through the teaching and guidance of the Holy Spirit, we become the redeemed son or daughter of God. Having learned who we are in Christ, and how to put on the mind of Christ, we become able to do **the same works Jesus did.** It's **not** because we are so **great**, but because we honor the fact that the Great and Holy God lives within us, guiding and empowering us by His Holy Spirit (His Will).

Speaking to sickness, injury, or disease, and commanding in the name of Jesus for it to depart, requires being a **believer** who knows who they are in Christ! Likewise casting out demons, even satan himself, commanding in the name of Jesus they go back into Hell, requires being a **believer** capable of putting on the mind of Christ. Still success requires our motive for doing such works is not to being us acclaim. But rather because we love those who are sick, diseased, or injured, and those possessed by demons, the same as we love ourselves.

If it were we who were in need of healing or deliverance, would we not desire to find someone who would love us enough to bring what we were in need of? We then, must choose to do likewise. Knowing who we are in Christ is the brand new beautiful car, being able to put on the mind of Christ is the powerful battery, loving others as our self is the fuel. But loving others as Jesus, is the engine which makes it happen.

Now let's explore the ability of doing even **greater works** than Jesus did. What might they be? Never once did Jesus open spiritually blinded eyes, nor spiritually deaf ears, that they might see and hear, as I've said before; He left that job for us to do as **believers**. It is pride which closes spiritual eyes and ears. Pride will not and cannot open any eyes or ears to the truth. Only by loving those walking in darkness, just as Jesus loves us, are we able by love, to reveal the truth of God's love and care for each soul. How are we are able to break satan's grip on our brothers and sisters who are walking in darkness? By the power of Agape' love being sincerely offered to them.

Far too often people in the world have witnessed only the religiously proud, desiring not to lead others into the Kingdom of God; but into the pride and label of their "religion." I know when I was a "Catholic," we were taught to pray for those ignorant people of other labels, such as Baptist, Presbyterian, Episcopal or any other equally "religious" bunch. We were taught only to pray for them to be led into the <u>one</u> <u>true</u> <u>church</u>, established by Jesus. Never were we encouraged to ask the Holy Spirit to help us be a witness to them. This was because the Holy Spirit was denied entrance into the rituals of the "Catholic Religion." Besides, we would be only asking that they trade one religious label for another.

I hope I have been able to shed some understanding on the ability of doing **Greater** works than Jesus did. Even though Jesus lowered Himself to receive the "flesh of man" when He became the second Adam, the works He did came <u>natural</u> to Him. But they are <u>unnatural</u> to us in our flesh, soul, and spirit. That is until we make the effort to learn from the Holy Spirit, who we are in Christ, and how to put on the mind of Christ. When we do this, even though it requires **great** effort on our part; such works can become <u>natural</u> to us. I'm learning to make the effort to cast out demons, **expecting** to see them flee. I am also learning how to pray for the sick, with **anticipation** of their recovery.

Could we ever thank Jesus enough for what He endured on Calvary for us? Never! But we may offer gratitude for restoring our relationship with our Father in Heaven, and giving us His Holy Spirit to dwell within our body, soul, and spirit, leading us into all truth. We do so by rejecting the lies, deceptions, and bondages of <u>religion</u>. We can seek daily the power to live as the redeemed son or daughter of God. We can also seek, if we already do not possess it, to receive from Jesus, the Baptism of the Holy Spirit and Fire.

✙ ✙ ✙ ✙

We daily can choose to crucify the will of our flesh that we may be led by the Holy Spirit in following Jesus. We can allow Him to lead us into edifying the Body of Christ, by the unifying power of Love. Lastly, we can seek the power to do those **greater works**, by working to attain mature faith - spiritual maturity.

God does not even ask or require this of us. **But to as many as receive Him, He gives the power to become the sons of God, even to those that "believe" on His name"** (John, chapter 1, verse 12). God never forces us to use this power, that we may **"become"** His son or daughter.

But when He can see us seeking to know how to use this power, by the teaching of the Holy Spirit; and when He sees us seeking spiritual maturity as a worthwhile goal to attain, it delights His heart. For in seeking spiritual maturity in our relationship with God, we are truly seeking first the Kingdom of God (Luke, chapter 12, verse 31). When we do this, rejecting powerless religion becomes as natural as breathing. We can prove to Jesus that we truly are His disciples, a Christian, a "follower of Christ." With the Holy Spirit's guidance and the Fire of Jesus' Love inside, we can and **will** win the world to Christ! Amen!

CHAPTER FIFTEEN
THE VOICE OF ONE CRYING IN THE WILDERNESS OF RELIGION

Awakening one morning, I was pleading with the Holy Spirit to help me get the job I have been given, done right and soon. My job is to help the bride of Christ prepare to be worthy to receive her Groom. The ONLY bride worthy of receiving Jesus is one which knows how to love others, the same way Jesus does. A bride not just talking and preaching about loving others like Jesus loves us. But one bold and bright, with daily actions of Jesus' kind of love extended toward EVERYONE!

Often I have felt as if I were some sort of modern day John the Baptist. Hearing almost daily ministers preaching, "Jesus will be returning any day now – look at the signs!" Whenever I hear such a message, in my spirit I cry out saying, "Jesus does not have a bride worthy to return for! Where is the unity in Love which He asked the Father for His bride to possess and show to the world? Those in the world do not know Who Jesus is; by Whom He was sent; and Why He was sent – simply because the religious are uninterested and/ or unable to answer the prayer Jesus prayed. It is far easier and more fun to criticize and put down one another, due to differences in man-made doctrines, traditions, and dogmas of prideful Religion.

As I stated in the introduction, I feel as if I am the voice of one crying in the wilderness, saying "Bride, prepare to be worthy!" Yes, there is coming a day when the True Bride of Christ shall arise. But she will not be made of "Religious" people. They are the "Lukewarm," which we are warned will be vomited out of His mouth when Jesus returns for His bride to join Him in the clouds. The TRUE Bride of Christ will consist of the wise virgins; those having a full supply of the oil of the Holy Spirit and the Light provided by the Fire of Jesus' kind of Love to light the way to meet her Groom.

✝ ✝ ✝ ✝

The unwise virgins are those caught up in "religion," possessing a "religious" spirit. They follow after a religion made from satan or the flesh, rather than the Holy Spirit of God. The oil in their lamp will run out because they have only a form of Godliness. Depending on the weakness of man, they deny the Power needed to truly live a Godly life of righteousness, peace, and joy. This is because their "Religion" has placed a vale over their spiritual eyes. They have failed to ask and permit the Holy Spirit, and He alone, to be the source they draw truth from.

When Jesus returns to claim His bride, the wise virgins will have a full supply of the guidance and the Power of the Holy Spirit in their life. Their lamps will be full because they daily choose to crucify their flesh, gladly yielding their spirit to the guidance of the Holy Spirit; seeking His wisdom and discernment, not that of man. They will follow the right path toward the Groom, because the Fire of Jesus' kind of love resides within them. This Fire will light their way to meet Jesus in the clouds when He calls.

What I am now going to share may offend some pastors, though it is not my intention to offend, but to enlighten. The Holy Spirit revealed to me that constant preaching of Jesus' return any day now is only preparing hearts to be easily deceived by the many false messiahs which will precede Jesus' return. Being too anxious for that day of Jesus' return, will cause many to fall for imitation messiahs who will proclaim they are Jesus.

God's Word tells us to be anxious for **nothing**. Nothing would include the return of Jesus. I say to you by the anointing of the Holy Spirit, be <u>ready</u>, be <u>prepared</u>, but be not anxious! Joyfully await the day of Jesus' return, but wait as a good and faithful servant. One who is diligently working each day to harvest spirits in the field of the world; await as one excited about the hope of what a wonderful day that will be - not anxious about knowing the time or the day.

✟ ✟ ✟ ✟

Indeed, we see many of the signs of the last days, what is good being called evil; while what is evil is being called good. We can see evil abounding daily, as the hearts of many have waxed cold, The acceptance of **abortion** and of what is called, "alternate lifestyles" as <u>normal</u>, are perfect examples. But what have we to fear? For where sin and evil abounds, how much more will God's Mercy and Grace abound! The deeper the darkness, the greater the Light will shine!

Instead of <u>looking</u> for signs, the Holy Spirit would have me tell you to BE A SIGN! Work with the Holy Spirit to reject any and all of man-made Religions' doctrines of pride and division. Come together in Love, through the Fire of Jesus' kind of Love alive within your body, soul, and spirit! Each day learn to appreciate and enjoy the "Relationship" Jesus came to restore with our Father in Heaven and each other. Work with the Holy Spirit to bring an answer to the prayer Jesus prayed for His church, His bride. Become <u>ONE</u> in the <u>Unity</u> <u>of</u> **LOVE**!

If you still wish to look for a sign, LOOK FOR THE SIGN OF THE HOLY SPIRIT BEING POURED OUT UPON ALL FLESH! Let those in the world no longer find reason to call Christians just another of the confused "Religions" in the world. Let us strive to permit those in the world to gain the ability to differentiate between those having only the powerlessness of label wearing "Christian" Religion; and those possessing Powerful Relationship with their Heavenly Father. Let them know we are the redeemed of the Lord, and have used the Power within (the Holy Spirit) to **become** the spiritually mature sons and daughters of God we were intended by God to be.

No longer babies or children being tossed to and fro by every doctrine of "Religion!" Let those in the world be in awe as they see **believers** healing the sick and casting out demons in the name of Jesus! Observe the raising the dead, both spiritually and physically, back to life. This is how the early church grew in numbers daily. This is how the Bride of Christ should be in the world of today and tomorrow, as we receive the Powerful outpouring from God's Holy Spirit!

In the early days of the church, such activity continued until "religion" began to water down the truth regarding the Good News, and began denying the Holy Spirit to be the One to lead and teach those seeking to follow Jesus into ALL TRUTH. "Religion" was created by the Pharisees within the early church. It has expanded throughout the ages due to mans fleshly lust for power. Yet without the Spirit of Truth to draw from, religion is empty and powerless. It has nothing of everlasting spiritual value to offer. The peace it offers is a false peace – not the Peace found by possessing within, the Kingdom of God.

Only the "Relationship" Jesus came to restore, offers knowledge concerning the fullness of the Godhead – Father, Son, and Holy Spirit. With such knowledge in your possession, though satan will try, he cannot deceive the "elect" of God. The "Relationship" Jesus restores by His blood and through the indwelling presence of His Holy Spirit, allows us to know Righteousness, Peace, and Joy. As we seek for the Holy Spirit to teach us to know who we are in Christ, and how to put on the mind of Christ, we will become the kind of **believer** capable of doing the same works which Jesus did.

As we feed on God's Word under the influence of the Holy Spirit with spiritual hunger and desire for spiritual maturity, we will become the kind of **believer** who will actually be doing even greater works than Jesus did. How? As we become prepared to always and instantly give reason for the Hope and Joy our faith brings, spiritually blind eyes will become open to see the truth, spiritually deaf ears, will be opened to not just hear, but <u>listen</u> to the truth.

All Pastors and teachers working in the ministry who are truly called by God, not self – please hear what the Holy Spirit would have me say to you. Stop exciting your flock about the soon return of Jesus. I would caution you instead, <u>prepare</u> them to be the bride worthy for Jesus to receive unto Himself. <u>Teach</u> – but seek to teach <u>ONLY</u> under the guidance of the Holy Spirit, and not your flesh. Allow the Holy Spirit to create the desire in each member of your church to learn from Him who they are in Christ, and how to put on the mind of Christ.

Please hear what I said. <u>Let</u> <u>the</u> **Holy Spirit teach** <u>such things</u>! He is the source of oil by which our lamp will remain lit. I had asked if I might teach on such things, when He first revealed to me such need among God's sheep. His answer to me was **NO!** The Holy Spirit told me it was His work to reveal this teaching to each heart individually, that diligently will seek to learn. Likewise, it is His job to teach each of us how to be holy, as our Father in Heaven is Holy.

Our job as followers of Christ (Christians) is to reveal to all, who we are in Christ, as we lay hands on the sick and pray for their healing. Our job is to prove we have on the mind of Christ, as we go about casting out demons whenever the occasion to do so arises. Our job is to reveal our desire to follow Jesus faithfully, when our lifestyle reflects a true concern for holiness, rejecting immorality in any form, and demonstrating that the Spirit of God is in control of our life. This can and will happen, if we daily die to self, crucify the will of our flesh, and are willing to make a sacrifice of Love (take up our cross) following Jesus, as the Holy Spirit guides us.

Fellow ministers of the Word of God, our job is to ask the Holy Spirit to help us prepare the Bride of Christ to be worthy. Our job is to work toward answering the prayer Jesus prayed to His Father for unity. We must work toward uniting with other **true** members of the body of Christ, with a genuine love for one another. There is a false body of Christ - it is those following after prideful religious doctrines of division, created by satan and man. The true body and bride of Christ is found among all who are led by the Spirit of God into all truth, and into sharing the Loving "Relationship" which Jesus prayed they would have among one another.

In closing, I would say, don't teach about Jesus returning any day to call His bride to join Him in the clouds. Instead, teach how to be a bride worthy of Jesus returning for. Teach how important it is to be ready every day to meet our Heavenly Father on the Day of Judgment. Teach how we may enjoy the loving relationship Jesus desires us to have with Him, our Father, and the Holy Spirit each day of our life. Teach how to seek possessing discernment that our spiritual ears are open to hear and listen to only the voice of the Holy Spirit each day, as we choose to dwell within God's Kingdom. Teach about the hope we have in knowing our Savior will be standing beside us when we face the Judgment of our Father in Heaven.

We all must remember what Jesus asked three times of Peter. **"If you love Me** – (you will) **feed My sheep."** We as ministers of the Gospel of Jesus Christ must seek wisdom, guidance and discernment from the Holy Spirit; that what we teach always will "edify'" the bride and body of Christ. Let us seek to avoid our flesh, satans' or the worlds' wisdom, getting into anything we offer as food fit for the perfection of the saints. The old saying: "practice what you preach" contains much wisdom.

If we constantly seek to preach by the influence of the Holy Spirit, we will be leading God's sheep to walk daily in the Spirit; dwelling within the Kingdom of God. This is the job assigned to everyone called by Jesus to feed His sheep. We must be very careful about what we feed His sheep, only that which comes from His Word, by His Spirit, is food fit to equip the saints of God for victory!

I pray this message has been of benefit to you. It has been to me. Any who might have initially gotten angered may now have come to a place of agreement as to why the Holy Spirit instructed me to speak so boldly. The job assigned to each of us is very important for the times in which we are living.

The "Religious" crowd will continue attacking me for exposing their games of lies and deceptions worked upon the hearts of those seeking to know, love, and serve God. Although they wish to rant against what the Holy Spirit has revealed, I pray many choose repentance for having allowed "religion" to lead them astray from the guidance of the Spirit of Truth.

CHAPTER SIXTEEN
WHY IS THE TRUE BODY AND BRIDE
SO SMALL IN SIZE?

This is the question I brought before the Holy Spirit out of curiosity. The answer I received was clear and made sense. You see, after over 2,000 years since Jesus established His church, which is made of true "believers" (those able to do the same works Jesus did, and even greater works); I thought the church should have grown to major proportions in the world by now. But as we know, sadly this is not so. Why not? I asked of the Holy Spirit.

Let's start by looking at a basic fact. Jesus proclaimed that the gates of hell would not prevail against His church. Prevail, does not mean satan would not wage war against the true body and bride of Christ. It simply means, <u>never</u> would satan win any war against the true body and bride of Christ. satan cannot ever be victorious over the true body and bride of Christ (which consists of true believers). Why would this be so? Because the true bride, not operating under the bondage of religion, but being guided by the Spirit of Truth, has sought after and received, the Promise of the Father.

Herein is the problem, it is found in man-made religion. Fearing the Spirit of Truth because of His exposure of their use of twisted scriptures and false, man-made teachings; religion refuses to allow its followers to believe in or go after receiving the Promise of the Father. Religion will teach, that was only for those 120 back then, no longer is it available for you and me. Having spiritual eyes and ears which are blind and deaf, the followers of "christian religions" readily accept this lie. Therefore they believe it would be a waste of their time to even pursue receiving such power from Jesus.

✚ ✚ ✚ ✚

This obvious lie has stunted the spiritual growth of many who believe they are serving God to the fullest. There are so many gifts of spiritual power available to those receiving the Baptism of the Holy Spirit and Fire. But sadly, religion denies belief in their existence. When they encounter one who has the ability of demonstrating the power of God in their life; religion tells them such a person is under the deception of satan. It seems as if having power emanating from the Holy Spirit, makes one delusional in the eyes of those possessing only "christian religion."

Looking at the facts, for centuries bigoted, prideful, unloving and divisive versions of "christian religions" have given satan material to feed those in the world the idea that Jesus, the Son of God, and Savior of the world is not for real. Powerless, judgmental and unloving label wearing, spiritually blind and deaf people, using the name "Christian," have caused many an atheist and agnostic to find no reason to trust in Jesus or in His Gospel. Can you imagine how sad this makes God? The gates of hell do prevail over the false church and its members which possess and rely on powerless man-made teachings of bigotries, pride and division. The gates prevail, by the permission of religious lies to stand in authority, denying the power God would give to all who seek to receive from and be led by His Spirit of Truth. The gates of hell prevail, because as with the Jews, a veil is placed over the spiritual eyes and cotton is stuffed in the spiritual ears of the followers of <u>any</u> and <u>every</u> man-made "religion," be it called Christian or not!

Remember, those who started out as the "chosen people" of God? Using man-made laws, doctrines, and traditions, along with twisted scriptures, the Scribes and Pharisees turned the "chosen people" of God into their "religion." Because of having chosen to follow after "religion" with its false teachings, they could not recognize their promised Messiah, even when He walked among them, teaching the "good news" regarding the Kingdom of God now becoming available to mankind.

The times before and after 9/11/01

If I may, please allow me to take you back to the days before 9/11/01; then we will look at what has happened in the years since 9/11/01. If you recall, before that hate filled day, in which those in service to satan committed evil, inhuman acts of cowardice; many church buildings were sitting empty. Many church buildings had gone up for sale. Then satan's attack came upon America. How quickly churches became filled, as people eagerly sought to find the One True God. I mean the One True God, Whose protection America was founded to be under.

Magazine covers and news reports displayed formerly nearly empty church buildings becoming filled. But how long did that phenomenon last? Not all that long. Once again today, many church buildings sit empty or are placed for sale. Why did that happen? Simply because those returning to church after years of absence, soon came to realize the reason why they had dropped out in the first place – powerless "religion" was all that was being offered. Those "christian" churches which fear the Spirit of Truth, were offering only man-made junk food to their listeners. Those seeking to know and hear the truth quickly will become disenchanted with half truths using twisted scriptures, man-made doctrines of pride and division, and just plain lies and hypocrisies.

Deciding such nonsense was not worth wasting their time, again many dropped out from attending church. Sadly, many are still unaware of churches where the Holy Spirit is permitted to take over and lead the service. Such churches are full of power, as the Spirit of Truth is welcomed into the hearts of the followers not of "religion," but of their restored "relationship" with their Father in Heaven. Many become discouraged by man and satan, and fail to continue seeking to find a church offering the Spirit of Truth.

Era of Mega Churches

satan is always ready to offer his alternative to comfort and mislead the masses. Today, we have what is known as the Mega church. Thousands of followers are attached to these ministries. Affable and well versed "men of God" are speaking to a crowd of people who desire finding "user friendly" churches. There is more than one way to reach Father God. Jesus alone is not the "only" way. What about the gifts and fruit of the Spirit? Pursue them if you wish, or ignore them, if they are too great a burden.

Once when looking to find a church to attend, I came across the pastor of such a church. In speaking with him over the phone, as a new perspective member, I asked several questions of him. With one, I was sly. In a sarcastic voice I asked, "Do you believe in this speaking in Tongues?" His answer exposed the user friendliness of his church. "Well,

I don't make an issue of that. We have some members who do believe in that, while others believe it is of the devil. So I do not bring up the subject, least any be offended." He went on to declare, "I myself have that gift, but I don't push it on others, I let each decide for their self."

I then asked, "Do you believe God gave you this gift just to use for yourself, or to share with others? Isn't it your job as a minister to clear up misconceptions and lies of satan, and help empower those seeking to be followers of Christ with the gifts available to them?" He then asked me if I was a minister. "No, I'm only a Christian author," was my reply. "Well, it sounds to me like you should be a minister. You may be missing your calling." Sadly, after saying this to me, he went on to tell me how he believed I would not be happy attending a "user friendly" church like the one he ran. He was honest, and he was right!

✟   ✟   ✟   ✟

What is one to do in today's world so filled with religions? When one desires to know the truth, and be led by the truth alone, how do you cut through the confusion and man-made lies? Seek to know, love, and serve, only the One True God. But seek this will all of your being. Seek Him daily and into the night! You may be asking, why? It is because God is a rewarder of those who diligently seek Him. Ask also, for the wisdom and guidance of His Holy Spirit, to direct you to a Spirit led church, and to give you discernment, so as not to be deceived by what you find.

If you find yourself belonging to a church which tells you not to bother pursuing receiving from Jesus Himself, the power of the Baptism of the Holy Spirit and Fire; you are as lost and powerless as those being taught to pursue darkness, despair, and both spiritual and physical death, hating any not of your "religious beliefs."

I know I have stepped on some toes. But how about this, are you willing to take accountability for the spiritual choices you make? You may as well say yes. As on the day of Judgment God will hold you personally accountable. If you are, may I challenge you to make a valuable decision? Why not go after receiving the Baptism of the Holy Spirit and Fire? Diligently and sincerely petition Jesus to show you this **is** available. Do this tirelessly, until you receive. I ask this of you, because if you seriously will take my challenge; the true body and bride of Christ will grow, and the "religious," false body and bride will diminish.

Ask yourself, what do you have to lose? Only powerless religion! What have you to gain? The wedding garment and the ability of being invited to attend the wedding feast of the Lamb. But even more, you will have spiritual power to defeat the gates of hell. Find a Spirit filled and led church to attend today. I'm speaking of one not only encouraging you to seek the Baptism of the Holy Spirit and Fire. But one also offering to help teach you how to do so. However, beware of those who mistakenly associate speaking in tongues as having received this blessing. This teaching is false and misleading, for that is not what the Promise of the Father is about.

The promise of the Father is about the answer to the prayer Jesus prayed to the Father, concerning His bride. Those who receive the promise of the Father, make it possible for Jesus to finally be able to find a bride which moves in the unity and power of Agape' love; a bride worthy for Him to receive unto Himself. Selah!

CHAPTER SEVENTEEN

GOD OF WAR, GOD OF LOVE
AND PEACE, GOD OF WAR

It recently occurred to me that I know mainly the God of the New Testament. Always I have found the most encouragement, spiritual strength, and knowledge, through partaking of the Word of God within the pages of the New Testament. II Corinthians, 3:6, tells of my gifting from God as an able teacher of the New Testament. The ways in which I have come to know the personality of God are: first, God is Love! Secondly, God's love for us is PERFECT! He proved this by sending us His only begotten Son to suffer and die in our place on a cross at Calvary. God seeks for us to forgive others, as He forgives us. Jesus commands that we love others the same way He loves us, which is: UNCONDITIONALLY!

When we attain the power of loving like this, as exemplified by Corrie Ten Boom's testimony, there is no offence for which we cannot find forgiveness in our heart, to offer the offender. Most of us haven't gotten that far as yet. Religion has not access to the wisdom of the Holy Spirit, to be able to

teach how we may attain the power needed to love unconditionally. The purpose of this book is to share how we, as
the **true** body and bride of Christ, may arise in power, the
power of Agape' love; come out of the world, and sincerely
love others, as Jesus did, into the Kingdom of God.

But in looking back to the Old Testament days, we so very
often see a God of War. A God Who on occasion seemed to
lack mercy, love, or compassion on His enemies. I can remember one occasion where God commanded Jewish King
Saul to slaughter not only all of the Amalites, but their slaves,
servants, and all the livestock they possessed. What had servants and slaves to do with warring against God and the
Jews? I asked. Why slaughter non-combatants who had no
choice? Why must they be punished when they had no say in
the matter? This seemed a bit harsh; even their animals had
to be slaughtered to the last one.

✠　✠　✠　✠

It appears to have been a test of obedience, which Old
Testament records reveal King Saul and Israelites badly
failed. We know they could not resist the temptation to
claim some animals as spoils of victory, even though God
had said, "No!" Because of their obvious disobedience, God
severely punished King Saul and the Israelites. In looking at
the recorded history of the people of God, slaughter of their
enemies with God's help ranks often and high among their
list of accomplishments.

I have heard that the harshness of God in dealing judgment upon His enemies was because the time of dispensation had not as yet arrived. Jesus had not come to complete
His mission as Messiah.

Jesus, the One Who brought mankind a means of es-
caping the wrath of God, offering hope of renewal of the
Relationship – not religion, which Adam and Eve, through

sin had lost. Becoming born again (by the Holy Spirit of God), we could now once more be what God had created us to be, His children. He empowers us with His Kingdom, giving us the power of abundant living, with Righteousness, Peace, and Joy within, along with His Will – His Holy Spirit, to help guide us into growing up spiritually, to <u>become</u> the redeemed <u>sons</u> and <u>daughters</u> of God (John 1:12).

The day of dispensation had arrived! But evidence from the Old Testament days of following after "Religious practices" taught by the Scribes and Pharisees, were exposed by Jesus as not coming from the heart of God. A woman caught in adultery was brought before Jesus by an angry crowd. They angrily demanded of Him that the Law of Moses prescribes she be stoned to death. Boldly, with self-righteousness they asked of Jesus: "What do You say?"

As we know, at first Jesus failed to respond. Seeming to ignore their question, He simply began writing on the ground. What He wrote is not recorded, but I believe it was the true law of God – the Ten Commandments. Then Jesus responded by picking up a stone. This action aroused the crowd's passion for blood even more. Jesus then issued a firm challenge to the crowd. **"Let he among you who is without sin, cast the first stone!"**

✠ ✠ ✠ ✠

At this challenge, those in the crowd began to read what Jesus had written on the ground. It is recorded, that one by one, from the oldest to youngest, they dropped the rock they were holding, quietly and humbly they walked away. **"Where are your accusers now?"** Jesus asked of the woman at His feet. Looking around she exclaimed, "They are gone Lord." Then Jesus said to her, **"Neither will I condemn you. Go your way, and sin no more."** This event displays the Love, Mercy, and Compassion of God, as ministered through His Son, Jesus.

As we read through the New Testament, we find many more examples of a God of Great Mercy, Grace, and Love. When asked of Jesus: "Teach us how to pray?" Jesus began by calling God, our <u>Father</u>. From the beginning of the ministry of Jesus, to this very day, the Good News is to be declared to mankind. What is the Good News? The Kingdom of God (Your inheritance obtained by restored Relationship) is available to you who are lost and have been displaced by sin. Forgiveness and restoration is available to you, by the sacrifice of Love made by Jesus on the cross for your sake. Be no more people who walk in darkness, fear, hatred, and evil. No longer be slaves to the devil, become the redeemed of the Lord! Choose to walk daily in the Light of God's Love!

The opportunity of being embraced by God's Mercy, Grace, and Love is yours for the taking. You need no longer be living under the judgment and wrath of God, but under the **unconditional love and forgiveness** of your Father in Heaven. Now you may walk daily within the Kingdom of God, dwelling in the Secret Place of the Most High! Today, all of these blessings and many more are made available to whosoever will. Will do what? Repent sincerely of every sin in their life; seek and acknowledge Jesus as Lord and Savior; believing in their heart Who He is, and speaking with their mouth to others, telling of the mission of the Messiah having been completed in your life.

✟ ✟ ✟ ✟

As we read the signs of the prophets today, we can see those days of dispensation are nearing an end. The harvest, as Jesus proclaimed, is so plentiful. But the workers indeed are few! It is time for the True Body and Bride of Christ to do the work required of them. Become bold soldiers and harvesters of spirits within the world. Using the Sword of the Spirit skillfully, under the guidance of the Holy Spirit, motivated by Love, be that LIGHT of LIFE to a world in darkness, a Beacon of Hope for all mankind! Come out from among the world, and make evident to all that you are not powerless "religious" wimps, but the redeemed sons and daughters of the Lord! Let the redeemed of the Lord say so – by their words and in their actions of Agape' Love!

Please hear the voice of one crying in the wilderness of man and satan's "Religions"! Never fear to take your bold and righteous stand against the forces of darkness. Love your brothers and sisters enough to not desire seeing any claimed by satan and his demons! Fight for their soul as if it were for your own! Love all who curse you, show mercy to those mocking you, and by the power of Jesus' name, cast out demons, sending them into the deepest pits of hell!

Religion will only allow you to fear doing such things. But by and through exercising faith in your loving "Relationship" with your Father in Heaven, with His Holy Spirit living inside, and in the power of Jesus' name, you can and shall do such things easily.

True bride of Christ, the days are growing shorter. You must make yourself worthy to receive your Groom! Pay attention to the last book in the Bible, the book of Revelation. Quickly we are entering into such times as are foretold. The Bridegroom shall be returning to claim His bride from out of this world! The lukewarm, those possessing only powerless religion; because they failed to take God seriously, not being diligent in seeking Him nor His Holy Spirit that they may do His will, shall suffer through the times of harsh tribulation. Because God has warned, He will vomit the lukewarm out of His mouth (Revelations chapter 3).

✞ ✞ ✞ ✞

When Jesus returns in Glory with His army, the world once again will see the **God of WAR!** The time of dispensation shall have been taken from the world in the rapture of the True Bride. In the time which follows, all whose hearts wax cold and chose to be enemies of God; all who unwisely chose to reject the Love of their Lord and Savior, mocking Him instead; shall see Him approaching on a white horse. A flaming two edged sword shall be in His mouth (the Word of God) as He makes war on demons, and the evil children of rebellion, disobedience, and darkness. It will be too late to seek Repentance, as Jesus annihilates every enemy of God from the face of the earth!

All reading these words need to be aware of one important thing. The words I write are not words of a fairy tale. They are words of Truth, inspired by the Spirit of Truth, found in the book of Revelation – the Word of the One, True, Living, God Almighty! I do not possess knowledge of you, nor what is in your heart. Only you and God know if you have truly chosen to receive or reject Jesus, the Son of God, as your Redeemer, Lord, and Savior. I do not know if you are presently caught in the deceptions of some powerless religion, be it called "Christian" or otherwise.

All I know to tell you is God truly Loves you. It is no accident you have opened and read this book with interest in what it has said. I am honored that the Holy Spirit has chosen to use me to write contents telling of God's unconditional love for you and me. Telling of how He desires to give us power of restored relationship with Him, as we choose rejecting religion. In love He offers us His Spirit and His Word. **"Man does not live by bread alone. But by every word which proceeds from the mouth of God!"**

✤ ✤ ✤ ✤

In closing I encourage you to feed daily upon the Word of God. By diligence and the Holy Spirit, plant it deep within your heart. In seeking the Power of the Baptism of the Holy Spirit and Fire, desire to become that pure, loving unconditionally, holy, and spotless bride Jesus is anxiously awaiting to return and claim as His own! Let the Fire of Jesus' kind of Love not only possess your words and actions. Seek for it to burn away all fleshly lust, desires, and impurities from your spirit.

Lastly, remember these words from God Himself: **"Many are called, but few are chosen."** Among those who desire to be called Christian, all are called to attend the Wedding Feast of the Lamb. But when the time comes for the Great Celebration; only those having on the wedding garment provided by the Father shall be allowed to enter into the hall of Heaven where the Feast shall be held. Those, whose garment is stained with "religion" or wrinkled by self-righteousness, will be denied entry. Those <u>chosen</u> to attend shall have on the pure and spotless gown of Agape' love, adorned with the Shekinah Glory of God.

CHAPTER EIGHTEEN
AS IN THE DAYS OF NOAH

The Word of God tells us that in the days preceding the return of Jesus, life in the world would be "as in the days of Noah." Matt. 24:37-51 "But as the days of Noe were, so also shall the coming of the Son of man be. For as in the days that were before the flood they were eating and drinking, marrying and giving in marriage, until the day that Noe entered into the ark, and knew not until the flood came, and took them all away; so shall also the coming of the Son of man be. Then shall two be in the field; the one shall be taken, and the other left. Two women shall be grinding at the mill; the one shall be taken, and the other left. Watch therefore: for you know not what hour your Lord does come. But know this, that if the goodman of the house had known in what watch the thief would come, he would have watched, and would not have suffered his house to be broken up. Therefore are you also ready: for in such an hour as you think not the Son of man comes. Who then is a faithful and wise servant, whom his lord has made ruler over his household, to give them meat in due season? Blessed is that servant, whom his lord when he comes shall find so doing. Verily I say unto you, that he shall make him ruler over all his goods. But and if that evil servant shall say in his heart, My lord delays his coming; and shall begin to smite his fellow servants, and to eat and drink with the drunken; The lord of that servant shall come in a day when he looks not for him, and in an hour that he is not aware of, and shall cut him asunder, and appoint him his portion with the hypocrites: there shall be weeping and gnashing of teeth." KJV

Although this is fairly descriptive, it got me to seek to know from the Holy Spirit what the days of Noah were really like. In reply, I could hear one word standing out among the rest, <u>Unrighteousness</u>.

I believe God would have us take a close look at the meaning of the word, unrighteousness. What does it consist of? Why is it wise to avoid it? Also, how may we avoid it?

I feel that in order to gain a comprehensive understanding of unrighteousness, we should first make the effort to grasp the meaning of its opposite – righteousness. Righteousness means we are living in right standing in the eyes of our Holy Father. No, not some guy wanting you to call him "holy" father, but the One and only, truly HOLY Father. Naturally this includes our having the desire to daily maintain and live a life pleasing to our Heavenly Father. In order for us to do this we must place God first in our life, by choosing to die to self, and crucify the lust and will of our flesh, that we may daily live and walk in the guidance of His Holy Spirit, as we dwell within in the Kingdom of God.

However in Noah's day, having and maintaining righteousness required having within, a strong desire to seek sharing a loving relationship with Father God, and desiring to better know, love, serve, and please Him everyday of your life. This is what set Noah apart from his contemporaries.

Such strong desires can only come from and be maintained by placing God and His ways first in your daily lifestyle.

From God's Word we learn that today, since the Sacrifice of Love made by Jesus on the cross in our behalf, our only source for obtaining righteousness is by receiving and being cleansed by the shed blood of Jesus. However in Noah's time, not having Jesus available to him; because of his desire to love, serve, please, and place God first in his life; God imparted it to him as righteousness.

We know that today, because of the work of Jesus on the cross in our behalf, all of our "good works" can no longer impart righteousness to us. In fact, all of our "good works" plied up over a lifetime, add up to the odor of a pile of dung – please excuse my direct use of vernacular. **Nothing** we could ever do could have the power and effectiveness to cleanse us from sin, as does the blood of our Messiah. Relying on your "good works" to gain entry into Heaven is based on false hope. It is a religious lie, taught by those not under the guidance of the Holy Spirit when interpreting the Scriptures; it is as simple minded a lie, as is being able to pray a loved one out of a place called Purgatory. How could a sinful person whose blood has no power, take precedence over the pure and holy blood offered by the Son of God, and Savior of the world?

Any who by the use of their spirit (their free will) chose to reject Jesus, and refused receiving Him as Lord and Savior, doing so upon their last breath, have willfully chosen to blaspheme the Holy Spirit. He is the Spirit of Truth, Who strove to reach hearts, seeking for them to receive Jesus, the Truth, the Way, and the Life.

When with your last breath, as God pulls your soul, made of His breath, from your body, you say no to Jesus, it is game over. There are no more chances to reject or receive Jesus into your life.

What about "good works"? Does this then mean we are not to be concerned with doing such things No indeed! It simply means placing upon them, their proper place and value in our daily life. Our good works should be motivated by our desire to not just **be** found righteous in our Father's sight; but to also **live** a righteous life for His honor and glory, and to show honor for His ways. When we choose yielding to the guidance of the Holy Spirit, that we may produce His holy fruit in our daily life; we are storing up treasures in Heaven if our works are motivated by sincere love.

Do you remember the rich young man who came to Jesus one day asking, "Good Master, what must I do to gain eternal life?" In response, we know Jesus spoke of several key commandments to obey. When the man answered and assured Jesus he had done so, Jesus did not rebuke him for lying. Instead, Jesus told him he lacked one thing. That thing was doing such works motivated by love, not to be seen by man, and receive praise from others for being a "good man."

However, going back to the days of Noah, Jesus had as yet come into the world, bringing the Light to know and see the Truth, the Way, and the Life to a world encompassed by darkness. So, not having the blood of Jesus available to him, was Noah a righteous man? The answer to such a question is both yes and no. I know this sounds both confusing and conflicting. Perhaps I'd better explain.

By today's standards, Noah could not be called a righteous man in God's sight. Indeed, in his day Noah had the same sinful nature as did his contemporaries. He had the same temptations to face, as did others of his time. Just as we all do today, due to the sinful nature we inherited from Adam and Eve's disobedience. Through Jesus, and the guidance of His Spirit within, we have the power to overcome that nature as we seek to become a new creation in Christ. We have freedom to crucify and put to death the old man, and walk in the newness of abundant life. We have ability to daily renew our mind, and to put on the whole armor of God, as we face our enemy, smiting demons with the Sword of the Spirit.

Although our brother Noah was not so well blessed as we, he chose nevertheless to be different from his contemporaries. Noah chose using his free will (his spirit), to fight against temptations to engage in evil practices, that he might life a life pleasing to Father God. Noah sought first daily, to live such a life before God and man. He did not know it, but he was seeking to dwell within the Kingdom of God.

Yes, the blood of Jesus was as yet available to Noah. But, because to God, Noah stood out like a beacon of light, in a world ensnared by darkness, God imparted it to him as righteousness in His sight. Apparently, Noah as Patriarch to his family, was such a good influence, setting such examples for his wife, family members, and their wives and husbands; they too sought to try being righteous in God's sight.

Noah could have fallen for satan's empty headed lie, as did most of his contemporaries. The lie which says, everyone is doing it, so why not me? I know in my past, I fell for that lie, as do many others. It makes you feel safe and secure living in your sin. How could it be so bad, when almost everyone else is doing it too? This bit of ignorant advice straight from the pits of hell, held most of Noah's contemporaries in bondage to sin and debauchery as it does in the lives of so many today.

✟ ✟ ✟ ✟

But I have discovered that in order to fall for this lie and not be able to see it for what it is, you must be willing to place God and His ways of Holiness, last on your list of priority things to do. To willingly commit to a life of sinful unrighteousness before your Holy Father in Heaven, you must show no concern for the very existence of God, or fear of His righteous judgment. Those who place their faith in such a simple minded lie of satan, choose to reject Jesus in favor of living a life devoid of true love. They become willing slaves to sin in all of its evil forms, as they permit demons to guide their every word and action. Is it any wonder God considers such to be among the unrighteous, when the time for judgment comes around?

We know that in the days of Noah, there finally came a day of judgment for the unrighteous. When that day came, only Noah and his extended family, along with the animals aboard, were spared from perishing in the great flood waters. Were it not for Noah's having been found to be a righteous man in Gods' sight, the human race as we know it, may have vanished from the face of the earth. God then would have to start all over from scratch.

Having created the first man in His image, perhaps in His second effort, God would have chosen to use the ape to work with. Thereby making the Darwin theory based in fact rather than in fiction. However, the very survival of Noah and his family, offers proof positive that such a theory is only based in fiction, not fact. Noah, and his family, survivors of the righteous wrath of a holy God, were made in His image, and not that of an ape! That is a fact of life!

I also find interesting, that the wages of sin paid by those who perished in the flood, are the same paid today by all who by their free will (spirit) choose to die rejecting Jesus. The reward for allowing satan and not the Spirit of God to guide your life is the eternal death and damnation of life in hell. Who in their right mind would seek such death, especially when God in His love sent us a Savior in His Son, Who suffered, bled and died in our place?

The Word of God tells us that after the flood, God repented of having caused those who chose living a life of unrighteousness in His sight to experience drowning in a flood. In my early days as a believer, I used to believe this part of Scripture, because of the use of the word "repented," meant God was sorry for His anger against those who chose to live for satan, rejecting Him and His ways of holiness. As I have gotten a bit older and mature, I came to realize, God had up to 40 days to "repent." Also, He is a just and holy God. Therefore His choice of dealing with the unrepentant sinner is just and holy. So what could the use of "repented" possibly mean, when applied to God in this part of Scripture?

As I have been seeking from the Holy Spirit, maturity, wisdom, and discernment; especially in the study of God's Word, that I might show myself approved, by the anointing of His Spirit of Truth, to teach from the Word; and as I have sought to become an oracle of God in what I speak or write, as God's submitted servant; I have been given a new and very sobering revelation as to the meaning of "repented" of having destroyed the world by flood. It is revealed by looking at the rest of this Scripture.

We know that in Mathew, as quoted, "as in the days of Noah" refers to how it will be at the returning of Jesus to claim His Bride to Himself. This Scripture offers evidence of the rapture of the true church and true bride of Christ. As it speaks of one taken and one left behind. In the days of Noah, once he and his family were safely inside of the ark, God Himself closed the door, and no one could open it. This was a form of the rapture, for all left outside the ark perished in the flood.

When we look at what God's Word goes on to tell us, after having spoken of God's repentance, the next time God chooses to bring judgment upon those choosing a life of unrighteous sin, and rejection of His Son, Jesus, it will be with the horror of a quick and painful fire! Fear alone, should make those rejecting Jesus to live a life of sin, consider and reflect upon the wrath and judgment soon to come from a just, holy, and loving God.

I ask that you only think about it for a moment. In the first days and weeks of falling rain, in the days of Noah, many found false hope by climbing to higher ground above the flood waters. Or perhaps they chose to cling to a passing tree trunk, and float along. However, as days passed on to over a month of nothing but rain. Having no higher ground for security or hope, they perished by drowning. Others, experiencing no nourishment for their body, lost the strength to cling to the tree any longer. They too perished in the flood by drowning. None could enter into the ark for safety, as there no longer was opportunity to repent of the sinful life they had led.

Can you imagine comparing that long, dragged out death, with all of its false hopes; to the awesome fear and pain of death as your flesh burns with fire unquenchable? There will be no offer of hope, only dreadful fear as the fire approaches. Will you be among those experiencing such a horrible end to their life?

In wonder, I asked the Lord about why such a quick, violent, and painful death, as consumption of our flesh by fire will be the means He will choose to judge those found unrighteous at the return of Jesus. The answer I received fits well with a just and holy God. The Holy Spirit told me that this time those found unrighteous; who chose flaunting such behavior before God, (such as promoting the murder of innocent babies for convenience, approving an abomination to God as just an "alternate lifestyle," etc. etc.) have chosen to do much more than just rejecting He and His ways of Holiness.

This time the rejection is much more serious, as all of these sins can be forgiven by sincere repentance and cleansing by the blood of Jesus. However, this time they have chosen to reject Jesus, God's only begotten Son. The One Whom He sent into the world to offer salvation to whosoever would receive Him. In His great Love, Jesus took upon Himself the suffering unto death, which we were due for our sins. Taking upon His holy self, the sins of the world, Jesus became sin for us, and our punishment from God was visited upon His loving body, to make our forgiveness through the sacrifice of His blood possible. Simply put, Jesus took our place on that cross at Calvary so long ago. But His blood never looses its power to cleanse us from any sin.

Yet even with all of this revealed; some who do not understand the nature of God would ask: How can a God of Love deal so harshly with sinners? Isn't He supposed to love the sinner but hate the sin? The answer is He does just that! But what of those sinners who choose to love unrighteousness, and hate the One sent by God to deliver them from it? Have they not chosen by such action to be worthy of the true, just, and righteous punishment of God? If the end comes, and they still refuse to call upon the name of Jesus, the answer has already been given. It was indeed their choice to receive the judgment of God. A decision made by exercising their free will (giving their spirit over to the guidance of the lust of their flesh and to satan and his demons).

Would you unwisely choose the rejection of Jesus? As the Bride of Christ becomes worthy for the return of her Groom, the days of Noah are rapidly coming upon us. Father God does not desire to see even one spirit perish and be condemned to the fires of hell. Because of this, and as proof of His great love, He sent Jesus to provide a means of salvation for His wrath upon sinners. Sincere repentance is the key to open the door of the Ark of the New and Everlasting Covenant, that God may fill it with His Spirit and presence.

Through receiving Jesus, our inheritance is restored, as we receive the indwelling presence of His Holy Spirit, as He brings with Him the Kingdom of God to be inside of us; and for us to be able to dwell within it. We are not given a spirit (will) of bondage (as in man's religion) but a Spirit of love, power, and a sound mind. Why would any fear having such a Spirit within? Especially as it is the Holy Spirit of God!

✝   ✝   ✝   ✝

Becoming born again by the Spirit of Truth, we receive the ability of discerning the lies of satan and man's religious teachings. He will lead us only into all truth. Man, by his religious doctrines, dogmas, and traditions of pride and separation, will only lead you astray from God and His ways.

Oh to become a new creation in Christ! To be able to daily live in righteousness, peace and joy in the Holy Spirit, as you dwell in the Kingdom of God while here on earth. To be able to be renewed in your mind, as you study the Scriptures not under man, but the same Spirit Who inspired their writing. What a Blessing! Living a life of spiritual abundance, a life having no fear, as you learn to fully trust in God's Perfect Love for you and me! Yes, my brothers and sisters I speak to you the truth, by the Spirit of Truth. You may escape the just destruction by the fire of God's wrath.

If you will only reject religion, and seek the restoration of your loving relationship with Father God and your brothers and sisters, through receiving Jesus as your Lord and Savior. Then you need only to ask, and seek with sincere and unrelenting diligence for Jesus to bless your life with the power of the Baptism of His Holy Spirit, and fill you with the Fire of His Love. He will do so.

Mans religion may even urge you to become born again by the Spirit of God. Then offer nothing else to seek from God, no power, no desire to do His will. They will even go so far as to tell you the power of receiving the Baptism of the Holy Spirit died with the last Apostle, long ago. That is a lie! Others, by the powerlessness of religion, will attempt to convince you that the Fire which accompanies the Baptism of the Holy Spirit, was and is, the ability to speak in tongues.

This is another man made misconception. All in their heart may mean well, but still the source of such misinformation is from hell! It is meant to keep the believer from becoming the kind of powerful witness of Jesus, which He said we could become!

✠ ✠ ✠ ✠

In closing, the Holy Spirit would have me ask of you, Where is your heart today? Is it caught up in the powerlessness of a man made religion, which fears the Spirit of Truth? Are you currently living among those in danger of perishing in the fire of the wrath of God? Or are you one living a life filled daily with the guidance of God's Spirit. If you do speak in tongues, do you use it wisely for the honor ad glory of God; or for self aggrandizement, as you show it off to others? Have you sought and received the Baptism of the Holy Spirit from Jesus, and the power of the Fire that enables you to love others as He loves you and me? The latter is my hope your answer contained. If not, I pray what you have read in this anointed teaching I have received from the Holy Spirit will encourage you to go after this wonderful blessing of power and hope in your daily life here on earth. This I ask for you in Jesus name. Amen.

CHAPTER NINETEEN
A PICTURE OF THE TRUE BRIDE
OF CHRIST

Today with so many last day prophecies being fulfilled, many are preaching the return of Jesus for His bride is soon approaching. But as I said in the beginning of this book, not so fast! Please tell me, where is the bride worthy for Jesus to return and claim for His Own? As I have stated, there is a <u>true</u> body and bride of Christ, and there is the false body and bride. The false body and bride are filled with twisted Scriptures and the prideful, powerless teachings of man's doctrines, dogmas, and traditions, which bring envy and strife. Its wedding garment is that of religion. On the other hand, the <u>true</u> body and bride of Christ is filled with and guided by the Spirit of Truth. Its wedding garment is made from having an Agape' love relationship with both God and man.

Looking at what I can see in the world today, the true body and bride of Christ has yet to get its act together. I boldly say this because the Holy Spirit has allowed me to see a picture of what the true body and bride of Christ looks like. God's Word tells us her wedding garment will be spotless. There will be no stain of man's religion or wrinkle of misguided faith upon the gown worn by the true body and bride of Christ.

The true body and bride of Christ, having sought after and received the Baptism of the Holy Spirit and Fire, will be daily demonstrating Agape' love toward all mankind. The true bride of Christ will have the ability and desire to answer the prayer Jesus prayed to His Father in her behalf. She shall be united by true, sincere, and "unconditional" or Godly **love**; not divided by pride in man made religious doctrines, dogmas, and traditions, having no foundation in God's Word or His Will.

✝ ✝ ✝ ✝

The true body and bride of Christ will know fully how to choose dwelling each day within the Kingdom of God. Every day she will be reaching out to those walking in darkness, offering them the opportunity to walk within the Kingdom of God. The true bride will have no fear of demons or satan himself! The true bride will be made of believers who not only will be doing the same works Jesus did, but those even **greater** works than Jesus did.

I spoke briefly about the wedding garment in the 10th chapter. Now I will attempt to give you the full picture I received. Once I was invited by a friend to attend a prophet's conference. I must admit I felt a little out of place, as this is not my gifting nor calling. My calling, as shown to me by the Holy Spirit, is that of a teacher to the true body and bride of Christ. Nevertheless, one of the leaders at this conference, a prophetess named Marilyn Smith, stated the Lord had allowed her to see the wedding garment which the bride of Christ will be wearing. She said it was the Shekinah Glory of God.

Upon returning home I spoke with the Holy Spirit regarding this revelation, and briefly, for a moment, I was allowed to see the same vision of the wedding gown Ms. Smith had spoken of. How bright, magnificent and pure the Light and Power of Unconditional and Perfect Love, which radiates from that gown!

Some may be unfamiliar with just what the Shekinah Glory of God is. I wanted to make sure I too understood what I had seen. So I looked it up in the Wikipaedia dictionary on the internet. I was amazed at what I found.

The word Shekinah does not formally appear in the Bible. Yet it is a Jewish word used to describe the presence of God which was with the people of God as they traveled forty years in the dessert. It was described as a pillar of fire by night, and a cloud by day. Once in the temple, the Shekinah Glory rested upon the Ark of the Covenant, which was inside the Holy of Holies.

✟ ✟ ✟ ✟

Get this! Even six times in the Quran, the Shekinah Glory is spoken of. It stands for peace, reassurance, calmness, and tranquility. Chapter 2, verse 248 states: "And their messenger said to them: Verily! The sign of His Kingdom is that there shall come to you At-Tabut (which stands for the lost Ark of the Covenant) wherein is Shekinah from your Lord and a remnant of that which Moses and Aaron left behind, carried by angels. Verily, in this is a sign for you, if you are indeed true believers." This is often described as the "reassuring feeling" of being in the presence (or under the protection) of God.

Is that not fascinating? The Moslems know of the Presence of God which rests upon the Ark of the Covenant. According to Moslem teaching in Ali ibn abi Talib, "Shekinah is described as a sweet breeze or wind, whose face is like that of a human." Too bad Moslems were not among the 120 gathered in the upper room on the day of Pentecost! "Suddenly, there came the sound as of a mighty rushing wind (the presence of the Holy Spirit)."

Let's take this idea of the Shekinah Glory and run with it, applying it to the true body and bride of Christ. She will stand out from the false bride, because her light will glow so brightly in a world filled with darkness. The Shekinah Glory of God shall be upon her, because the Power of God's presence will daily be made manifest in her words and actions of Agape' Love. Daily choosing to die to self, crucifying the lustful desires of her flesh, allowing her desires to come from the Spirit (will) of God; walking in the Spirit; she shall finally attain the power to be holy, as her Father in Heaven is holy, and to truly love others as Jesus loves her!

Have you seen this bride? Sadly, I think not yet. But God is choosing to use the foolish things to the world, such as me, to help the true bride arise and work to attain her full potential and worthiness to be given the wedding garment to wear; in order to be claimed by Jesus upon His return. Now as God is pouring out of His Spirit upon all flesh, there shall be a separation of the wheat from the chaff, a division of sheep from the goats. Soon, the false body and bride will fall in shame, as its folly is exposed by the light and love made manifest upon the true body and bride of Christ.

How is this to come to pass? Many may be wondering about this. First, we must come to understand that when we become born again of the Spirit of God through accepting the sacrifice of love made by Jesus, we are covered by His blood. His blood is what seals the New and Everlasting Covenant made by God with man. In it Father God says: He will write His commands on the hearts of His people, and their sins He will remember no more.

We, in having the Holy Spirit (Will of God) come to dwell within our body, soul, and spirit, become the Ark of the New and Everlasting Covenant established by God with His children. The Holy Spirit upon entering immediately writes the Commandments of God on the fleshly tablets of our heart. He is our Comforter, and teacher, Who when we ask and allow Him to, as the Spirit of Truth, will lead us into all truth. He is the One Which inspired the writing of God's Word. When we <u>study</u>, not just read the Word, He gives us the gift of discernment, that we may recognize false prophets, and teachers of "religion." Then using the gift of discernment, after trying the spirit, we choose not to follow their false teachings. God's sheep know His voice, and a stranger's voice they will not follow.

In my book: Ark of the New and Everlasting Covenant, I explain how when we become born again by the Spirit of God, we become that Ark, containing the New and Everlasting Covenant. Our body becomes the Temple of the Holy Spirit; our soul becomes the new tabernacle, not made by man. But in order for us to receive that part of the Promise of the Father which does directly effect us (In Jewish tradition, the father of the bride furnished the wedding garment), we must learn to make a daily choice in our spirit (our will). We must daily die to self, crucify the will and lust of our sinful flesh; ask for and yield completely to the guidance of the Holy Spirit (God's Will).

✟   ✟   ✟   ✟

Once we learn the importance and value of seeking first daily for the Kingdom of God to reign within our body, soul, and spirit; as we partake of the Baptism of the Holy Spirit and Fire, the Shekinah Glory of God will rest upon the tabernacle of the New and Everlasting Covenant; just as it did upon the tabernacle of the Ark of the First Covenant.

Earlier in chapter ten I stated it was the father of the bride who gave out wedding garments to the invited guests. So it is for the members of the true body and bride of Christ. We are told in the 14ᵗʰ verse of Matthew, chapter 22, that many are called, but few are chosen to attend the wedding feast of the Lamb. All who become born again of the Spirit of God are <u>called</u> to attend. But only those having on the wedding garment will be permitted (chosen) to do so.

If you attempt wearing the label of your "religion" as a proper garment, it will only get you thrown out in a very sad way. Do you remember what the father of the bride asked of the invited guest who chose not to wear the garment which had been provided by the father? "Friend, how is it you do not have on the proper garment?" A wedding garment had been given him by the bride's father, so there was no acceptable excuse to offer. Then the father said to his servants: "Bind him hands and feet, and throw him into outer darkness, where there shall be weeping and gnashing of teeth."

God's Word tells us that everyone is given a measure of faith.

Our job is to seek to learn from not man and his religious "beliefs;" but from the Spirit of Truth (Who will never lie, misquote or misinterpret Scripture, nor in any way lead us astray with false doctrine). We must ask for the ability to learn how to become the spiritually mature man or woman of faith, which God intends from the beginning for us to become. By the way, you can find this in John, 1:12. Sadly, not in the new watered down versions which will tell you that you are given the "right" to be a "child" of God. Or those stating that you instantly **become** a <u>child</u> of God, and may find comfort in staying that way for the rest of your life.

If you will but look at the King James version you will clearly see you are given the "ability" to "become" the sons (& daughters) of God. That ability is the indwelling presence and available guidance of the Holy Spirit. The words "to become" means you do not instantly arrive, but you must work at it, by surrendering your spirit (your free will), to that of God's will for your life (His Holy Spirit).

Another thing needed for the Bride to receive her wedding garment is, she must be in one accord. Being guided only by the Spirit of Truth, there will be no arguing over whose man-made doctrines and dogmas are correct; or whose light shines brightest. A servant's heart and humility is needed to surrender your life to the guidance of the Holy Spirit. To become capable, you must be willing to daily crucify the pride you have placed in "religious" dogmas, doctrines, and traditions, which do not please God. All who fervently seek to be worthy of receiving the wedding garment to be worn by the Bride of Christ for the wedding feast of the Lamb, will have chosen to reject man's "religion," to enjoy to the fullest, their restored "relationship" with Father God.

Are you one of God's sheep? Or has religion beguiled and led you away from the Spirit of Truth, using man-made doctrines, dogmas, and traditions of pride and division? Are you now, or would you like to become a member of the <u>true</u> body and bride of Christ? If your answer is yes, I would like to become a member of the true body and bride. Then you must stop attending a religious church, one denying you the teaching, indwelling presence, and guidance of the Spirit of Truth; one teaching you to rely upon the teachings of man and his twisted interpretation of Scripture. The honesty of your response will be demonstrated in your actions. You cannot continue walking in or supporting the lukewarm powerlessness of religion, and expect to have an ample supply of the oil of the Holy Spirit in your lamp when the Bridegroom arrives to claim His bride.

✟   ✟   ✟   ✟

I implore you to spend your life seeking to know to the fullest, the loving relationship with your Father in Heaven which

Jesus came to restore. Seek daily the power of the Baptism of the Holy Spirit and Fire to be within your body, permeate your soul, and ignite your spirit! Be quick to forgive others of any and every offense they may have committed against you. Seek to be able to love others the same way Jesus loves you. Wisely choose each day to dwell within the Kingdom of God. Do this at the start of each day, because in seeking first the Kingdom of God, everything you truly have need of will be provided for you by your Father in Heaven.

Surrender everything in your life to Jesus and the guidance of the Holy Spirit. Choose dying to self and crucifying the will of your flesh each day, that the Holy Spirit may help you to be holy, as your Father in Heaven is holy. We do this by asking the Holy Spirit each day to help us bridal our tongue, and lead us in walking within the Kingdom of God, as we choose to follow Jesus. Again I remind you that Jesus told us His sheep know His voice and a stranger's voice they refuse listening to or obeying. The voice of Jesus is the Spirit of God, which is the Will of God, known as the Holy Spirit.

Pastors, I speak now to you with the boldness of a messenger of God to the Bride. Do your part! Feed God's sheep the PURE Word concerning the Baptism of the Holy Spirit and Fire. Do so under the anointing of the Spirit of Truth, not relying on your own feeble ability! Do not preach based upon <u>wishing</u> for the soon return of Jesus for His Bride. Preach rather of <u>attaining</u> the <u>power</u> <u>needed</u> by His Bride, to make her worthy for His return! Your job and mine is to work toward seeing the True Bride of Christ receive from the Father, the wedding garment made of the Shekinah Glory. This should be the goal we work with the Holy Spirit to bring forth!

✟　✟　✟　✟

The Bride will no longer be looked upon by the world as a bigoted and powerless religious coward; but as a mighty warrior against the forces of evil. She will not release without a serious fight, the soul of any who are made in the image of God, whose soul was meant to spend eternity with God in Heaven! There is a bonus to be gained! When Moslems become able to see the True Body and Bride of Christ wearing the Shekinah Glory of God, they will flock to the One True God!

✝   ✝   ✝   ✝

Pastors please hear my plea! Work with the Holy Spirit to make of the true body and bride, those taught to daily carry and wield skillfully, the Sword of the Spirit. Teach how they may daily put on the whole armor of God, and dwell within the Kingdom of God while engaging in battles with the forces of darkness.

LET THE TRUE BRIDE OF CHRIST ARISE!

Let us work to put a smile upon our Father's face, giving Him reason to tell the hosts of Heaven to prepare a wedding fest for His Son. All who truly understand the messages found within this book, will not do works based on wishes for dreams to come true. Their work will be based on faith, that the Spirit of God will guide and empower them to become mighty harvesters of spirits in these last days. Mighty warriors in the Army of the One True God of Light, Life, and Love! They will not forsake assembling in churches where the Spirit of Truth has freedom to teach and feed God's children, sons, and daughters the pure and undiluted Word of God!

It is time now for me to end this book. But that does not end my heart's desire that the contents of this book, and boldness given me by the Holy Spirit, will make a mighty impact upon the lives of all desiring to belong to the true body and bride of Christ. May it help light a flame among members of the true body and bride of Christ.

ANSWERS TO THE CHALLENGES WHICH MAY COME

I know the contents in this book will be challenged by others, particularly among the "religious" crowd. I will be asked such things as, "How dare you write with such bold authority! Do you think you are God, or perhaps an Apostle? You claim you hear from God, by His Holy Spirit – REALLY!"

Among the religious there will be two different thoughts. One will simply state that I am an obvious nut case; as no one actually hears from God directly. The other will perhaps believe that I must be a very holy man, to receive such messages from the Holy Spirit. I know this is so, because during my days of being ensnared by religion, these would have been the two issues I would have been thinking about someone writing with such boldness.

The truth is I am neither a nut, nor any more holy than anyone else. I am a surrendered servant of God. Surrendered daily to the guidance of the Holy Spirit, asking daily to be able to hear His voice, as I choose to walk within the Kingdom of God, or as our brother David called it, the secret place of the Most High. All who have come to the realization that Jesus came for more then just the eternal salvation of our soul and spirit. But also to restore to purity in Father God's sight, the relationship with Him, which Adam and Eve originally possessed, before falling into sin, and taking on a sinful nature, through possessing the knowledge of good and evil.

With your relationship restored, and the gift of the Spirit of God residing within; hearing the voice of the Holy Spirit is a natural thing, once you have freed your spirit from the lies and bondages of man's religious ideas. Ideas which are based in pride and division, that leads you further away from knowing God, as He would have you know Him, by the leading of His Holy Spirit.

✝ ✝ ✝ ✝

Hearing the voice of the Holy Spirit has been a lifelong blessing for me. Since my childhood, I have sought to be a man like David, a man after God's heart, the apple of His eye. How I wish I could say that in hearing so clearly His voice, I never failed to follow through, and avoided sin in my life. But sadly, I must admit, were Saint Paul a contemporary of mine, I'm afraid I would take away the ugly title "chief of sinners" away from him.

Personally knowing what a failure to God I had been for decades, I prayed prayers of repentance to Father God. I knew my sins were many and were opposed to His holiness. Realizing I was the modern day version of what Paul once was, I began asking in my prayers, for God to do for me what He had done in Paul's life, turn it around, and make of me a man of God, whom He could mightily use for His honor and glory. No one was more in shock than me, when one day the Holy Spirit told me the work I have been given to do is help the true body and bride of Christ prepare to become worthy for Jesus to come back and receive to Himself.

In the flesh, this would be a frightening thing to be asked to do. In religion, I would have permitted satan to tell me I was far too "unworthy" to dare to even try doing such a thing. But I have finally learned in my spiritual life, to permit God alone to be my source. By His Holy Spirit, I am daily equipped for such work. It is not my ministry, but that of the Holy Spirit working through me. Therefore, I have no need to fear, or even to be discouraged by the uncomely rude comments which will be directed toward me by those lacking in understanding, being full of man's religion.

But here is the real **heavy** part of this ministry, if it be heavy. Every word of teaching within this book applies just as much to me, actually even more so. (To whom much is given, much is required). I, just like you, am seeking to be found among the members of the true body and bride of Christ. I also desire to be found wearing the proper wedding garment at the return of Jesus.

The teaching in this book applies every bit as much to me, as to anyone!

PREPARE TO RECEIVE YOUR GROOM!

This book is in no way an endeavor to write a new Bible. Every teaching within is backed by the Word of God! I challenge every reader to become familiar with the Word of God, that no false prophet may deceive you with lies and twisted Scriptures. Pray for daily, and use the gift of discernment. Use the Word of God to try every spirit, to know if it is of God. Asking for and using the gift of discernment, is so important for the times we are living in. May your life be blessed!

With love,

Carlote Bengemyer

MY REQUEST OF YOU, THE READER

I hope and pray the writings and powerful teachings in this book have helped in the depth of your spiritual walk. I rely totally on the Holy Spirit to give me the contents of each book of messages I write to the church. I know many of the "religious" crowd will hate me, and wrongfully call me a false prophet, when in reality I am a servant of God.

I am only answering God's call late in my life. It is by His mercy, grace, and love He has chosen to use me as He has. All praise, honor, and glory go to God alone for this! At present, I do not have much in the way of funds. In fact, I have no money to set aside to advertise this book to the church. Please understand, I am not seeking for anyone to send me any money at all.

What I seek is your help telling others about this book addressed to the TRUE Body and Bride of Christ. Would you please help me advertise, by telling others, or even purchasing copies to share with others? I have always believed that word of mouth advertising is the best kind which money cannot buy. Why? Because it must be earned by the quality it provides. If you find this work is of a truthful nature and is of quality; I pray you will deem it to be worthy for you to help me promote its existence.

I cannot bless you if you do, but I'm certain God could, according to His will. However, I choose not to curse you if you do not like the contents of this book, or even if you choose to curse me. I'd much rather forgive and love you as Jesus loves me. It is after all, the 11th Commandment of God!

www.ingramcontent.com/pod-product-compliance
Lightning Source LLC
Chambersburg PA
CBHW070105070426
42448CB00038B/1615